ur Spirits Up

"...mes it's more important than ever to help people develop
...ience and prioritise the things that really matter. This book
...ly combination of theory, examples and practical advice."
...nson, Director, Action for Happiness

"...al and useful book that will help anyone to get on top
... strains and struggles of everyday life. A valuable and
...tion that helps us realise that even if we're ticking along
...e in our lives, there are many things we can do to increase
...nd flourishing."
Founding Director, Capp, www.cappeu.com

"...k that inspires and challenges, as well as offering hope
...ce that it is possible to re-gain control of the way we
...dern day working practices. Wide-ranging and well-
...book blends science with real examples and wry humour
...or to our ways of working."
...ussell Foster, Oxford University and Chair of the
...cience Festival 2011

"...ike a very positive and down to earth approach to the
...esses that beset all professionals, with plenty of sound
...e on how to keep mind body and spirit together while
...eer, personal and caring responsibilities. Far too many
...ng people try to 'run on empty' instead of tackling the
...old us back. Good relationships, nutrition, exercise and
...step back for a moment and look at the big picture are
...y successful practitioner."
...rnold, Author, *Necropolis, Bedlam, City of Sin*

First published in 2011 by Creating Focus Publishing

www.creatingfocus.org

©Sarah Dale 2011

ISBN 978-0-9569169-1-4

Designed by Kate Ferrucci of Quarto Design

eping Your
Spirits Up

NS FROM THE CREATING FOCUS®
COACHING PROGRAMME

SARAH DALE

Creating Focus Publishing

To family and friends, especially Ingrid and Dennis.

CONTENTS

INTRODUCTION

One of the benefits of being a psychologist now firmly in middle-age is that I get to hear lots of insights and stories about what it means to be at this challenging, complex and often very rewarding stage of life. Despite the rather alarming experience of becoming a higher maintenance person than I have ever been (by which I mean feet, teeth and eyesight rather than anything more glamorous) as the years progress, I would not want to change places with my younger self. The hard won experience is worth something even if it does mean greater expenditure on things like moisturiser. I have a feeling that this is true for many of the people I listen to as well.

Who is this book for?

This book has been written for others of a middle-ish age (we'll leave the definition deliberately blurry – it seems to be more about a certain stage than age). Those who are likely to be well educated, successful in their careers, maybe professionally qualified too. Those who are also likely to have considerable responsibilities outside of work. They may have children, they may care for other relatives or friends and they may have extra voluntary jobs in or outside of work.

They are busy people who are achieving a lot but sometimes feel overwhelmed by their "to do" lists. They may be tired of the amount of change and uncertainty they have to keep dealing with. They may wonder what their next career or life move might be – and whether that move will be their own decision or the result of some possibly threatening change (such as redundancy) imposed upon them. They may even have experienced something of a traditional mid-life crisis (new motorbike or partner anyone?).

A note on mental and physical health

I am an occupational psychologist, not a clinical one. This means I do not specialise in diagnosing or treating severe mental health problems. I deal with people and their performance and well-being at work (which can encompass many factors). I am interested in both individual and organisational perspectives.

I am well aware that if you are experiencing severe depression or complex conditions such as bipolar disorder or chronic fatigue syndrome, this book may not be for you. The chances are you have tried many of the suggestions here and they may not have helped. In fact they may have made things worse by making you feel as if you have failed to help yourself in some way that you or others may expect, or by leaving you with great disappointment that your difficulties haven't gone away.

The last thing I intend is for anyone to use this book as a new way to beat themselves up for not coping in some way. Dealing with some of the challenges of mental and physical health (and the two are often deeply intertwined) can be a life's work, needing careful support from professionals and people around you and a clear awareness of what you need and what is in your own best interests. This book does not intend to replace any of that, and it is arguable whether any book on its own can be the answer.

What I hope this book can do

As an occupational psychologist, I am especially interested in what I call "sub-clinical" mental health. By this I mean that grey and widespread area which most of us experience at some time in our lives where we are functioning in our many roles, and coping. We may not be exactly thriving though.

This can be at an individual level or at an organisational one. Embattled organisations, tired of constant change and struggling with economic conditions can operate satisfactorily; but are probably not delivering truly great or consistent services or products. They may be staffed by people who likewise are working adequately, but may not be firing on all cylinders a lot of the time.

The vast majority of us cope well enough. We deal with work, family, responsibility, unexpected crises, finances, relationships, transition and ageing more or less successfully. We muddle through, we get by.

But we might not be enjoying it much. We might not be getting as much out of our work or life as we could, or contributing in as satisfying a way to our corner of the world as we know (or suspect) we could. There may be a lingering sense of "is this it?"

I should add that this is not about being perfectionist about our lives. I am not suggesting that we should all be operating at our full potential every day of our existence. In fact quite a theme of this book is about giving ourselves a break (literally and metaphorically).

It is easy to get into a vicious circle that means that: first, we realise how challenging things are; we respond by working harder to meet those challenges; we look after ourselves less well in the process; and then ironically become more stressed and almost certainly less productive. We can then find ourselves responding by trying even harder: by working longer hours, setting higher targets, multitasking on a grand scale. It can be a difficult cycle to break. I hope that this book can help to do that.

This book aims to address a whole range of areas that, taken together, can increase the chances of thriving rather than just surviving. Or if you feel as if you are drowning, to help you get to a state of mind that feels more like dry land. A calmer place to be where things are kept in perspective and better decisions can be made.

The book covers many different aspects of life, and aims to draw on research in a practical way. It is unlikely that one chapter alone is the answer to keeping your spirits up. For me, my family and my clients, it seems that a combination approach works best, and it is important to accept that it is an ongoing experiment to find the right combination at any particular time in your life.

It's not about aiming for a perfect balance. There is no such thing to my mind. It is more about being aware of what activities or habits might benefit from some tweaking. To understand more about any particular area, I strongly suggest you go to the books and websites referred to that go into more depth on specific issues.

Why did I write it?

The topics emerged as common ones through the coaching work I have done with people from a broad group of interesting people, often dealing with a great deal of change and uncertainty. I was writing brief "food for thought" articles to support my coaching programme (Creating Focus®) which pointed people to a few other books, ideas or theories that might be helpful in understanding what was going on for them. This book has grown out of those articles.

I began to realise that many of these people (including me as well) experience low to medium level anxiety from time to time. Whilst most present a genuinely cheerful face to the outside world most of the time, they do sometimes feel as if they are carrying quite a complex weight of responsibility and work load. This can threaten to crush their spirits on occasions – even when, fundamentally, they are very committed to and enthusiastic about their job and other aspects of their life. It then seems very common indeed that many of the strategies they have to keep themselves calm, focused, and in good physical and psychological health go straight to the bottom of the agenda.

This book aims to bring them back to the top.

CHAPTER 1

BEING OPTIMISTIC – AND GROUNDED

We need to stand

Mike and Bea Hunter run a small business called Better Languages, a translation agency based just outside Nottingham. The husband and wife team employ two others as part of their core staff, as well as managing a wide international group of freelance translators.

Featured on the business reality website, In a Fishbowl (www.inafishbowl.com), their highs and lows have been followed by thousands. And there have certainly been some setbacks. I had a long chat with Bea over a coffee about all this.

"I started this in the early nineties without realising I was starting a business. I did some translation and teaching at home whilst raising the children. Then Mike encouraged me to apply for funding to buy a computer, and I teamed up with an existing agency that then became ours. Better Languages in its present form was born.

"When Mike was made redundant from a senior management role in a housing organisation, he joined the company full time (bringing his new MBA with him), and soon it was doing well. We were profitable, still working from home, but had gained some great clients including a leading specialist children's retailer.

"So we decided to move into office premises, as we had outgrown home now we had two extra members of staff."

Bea smiles ruefully and shrugs as she goes on,

"Then we lost our biggest account through no fault of our own (it was owing to corporate decisions following restructuring of their business). And the recession started to hit our other clients hard."

Then – a huge blow to the close-knit company – one of the team had a sudden close bereavement.

Bea says, "By Christmas, the confirmed orders and cash flow were looking bad (though we were still getting lots of enquiries), and I was depressed. Mike was a rock. He kept saying 'we need to stand'"

Mike and Bea have complementary styles. Mike is more of a risk-taker whereas Bea sees herself as the more cautious and practical side of the partnership. This leads to an inevitable tension which can be very creative and keeps them both in the most helpful place to run the business successfully. As she puts it,

"When do you decide to hit the eject button? There is a critical moment when if you don't do it, it becomes too late and you risk crashing into the mountain. But if you do it too early or because you lose faith that you can turn the plane around, you may eject when you didn't need to."

One day in December Bea went to visit the accountant to talk about how to exit the business. Both she and Mike were tired and still hoping to find a positive outcome but the strain was building.

Within half an hour of getting back from the accountant, they received an order. In a strange twist of fate, it was the biggest one they had received since the previous financial year, by some margin. It put the conversations with the accountant on hold. It is a great illustration of the roller-coaster nature of small business, taking the emotions of the people involved with it.

Since then, things have been on the up. All the ground work of the networking, the good testimonials, the good relationships with major international clients are paying off. They are in the process of taking on a further member of staff (which they admit feels a bit scary).

Bea puts some of this turn-around down to her religious faith. It's not for me to argue with that but from my perspective I would put it down to the way in which they have dealt with setbacks: the support from each other, and, interestingly, the very conscious decision to trust each other whatever happens; the continued open communication – within and outside of the company; the building of a strong network; the cheerful (and honest) face they maintained to the outside world even when facing serious challenges; the perspective they gained from beliefs and activities outside work; the mindset they adopted when the chips were down.

As Bea says, "Confidence does not depend on success. You can succeed even when you are losing everything."

As we will go on to see, confidence and success are very often built on the things that seem like failures at the time. These are the roots of true optimism.

Stuff happens

This is not going to be a chapter about positive thinking. In fact I would go as far as to say that positive thinking *can* be a distinctly negative thing. Sometimes, positive thinking is the greatest form of denial. A blindly positive mantra that takes no account of the reality of difficult circumstances can be harmful.

It may mean we haven't assessed the situation or the risks we face wisely, and it may stop us from making the best decisions to deal with the reality.

It gives the sound research done under the banner of positive psychology a bad name. Positive psychology is not about pretending life is always positive. It is the study and practice of what makes people resilient and psychologically healthy (and very probably happier as a result) and grew out of a disenchantment with psychology as a field of clinical research that focused entirely on fixing what had apparently gone wrong with people.

- Things can and do go wrong.
- Things hurt: mentally and physically.
- We get disappointed, let down, we sometimes fail at what we set out to do.
- We can get made redundant.
- People we love can become ill or die.
- We can become ill or have an accident.
- Misfortunes happen to people who have done nothing wrong. And to those who have.
- We can be in the wrong place at the wrong time and get caught up in any number of wars, political unrest, economic melt-downs, accidents, disasters and general pestilence.
- It can rain on your parade.
- Life is not guaranteed to be fair.

How we react to the setbacks

When these things happen, we naturally have an emotional reaction. That's fine. In fact it's a good thing, if painful. The so-called negative emotions of fear, sadness, anxiety and anger all have their place, and it can be unwise not to acknowledge them when necessary. Bottled up or denied, they have a tendency to leak or burst out at some future unexpected point, often in ways we don't understand. Maybe even in physical ways, from headaches to more serious illnesses. Or they may get taken out on innocent bystanders.

People vary

It is clear, from our own observations as well as from psychological research, that people vary widely in how they respond to events. Put two people into the same situation and the chances are they will respond differently. The old thinking about various events or situations being inherently stressful had to get kicked out pretty quickly, although it is still an appealing idea to many.

The press can be quick to fixate on ideas such as labelling a particular Monday in January as more stressful than other days (there is no evidence for this), or that claim that moving house is more stressful than starting a new job for example. We may share feelings with other people about these events – but it is not the event *per se* that makes it stressful or not.

The inconvenient truth is that *I* may find giving a big presentation stressful; *you* may enjoy it. *I* may have no problem with travelling by plane; *you* may need medication to get you to the airport. *You* may be relieved to be made redundant; *I* may be terrified. We're all different (thank goodness).

There is more going on than the event itself. It is more to do with how we interpret situations. That inner voice constantly telling us *this* is good, *that* is bad; *this* is ok, *that* is threatening; *this* is enjoyable, *that* is frightening. Our personalities and experiences (nature and nurture) affect how we interpret events. How much control we perceive we have over a particular situation is a critical part of our assessment about how stressful it is. Life threatening events induce common reactions from many people (usually because we share a perception that we have very little control) – but even then, some of us seek out dangerous experiences (chasing natural disasters, extreme sports, being a bomb disposal expert). Threat and danger don't lead to the same behaviour from everyone.

It is important to recognise that the way in which emotions are felt or expressed will vary between people too. Some people cry easily, others don't. Some lose their temper easily, others don't. Forcing our expectations on others about how we think they *ought* to react can backfire. This has been found to be the case when studies of counselling immediately in the aftermath of some trauma revealed that this can do more harm than good if offered too soon or indiscriminately.

In relation to the less dramatic but still highly distressing events in our lives which we all experience at some time or other, we all make use of some strategies – which may be more or less effective – to return to our more normal functioning. This chapter aims to explore what is involved in the most effective strategies.

Bouncing back – or not

The key is not about avoiding or denying the difficult times in our lives. There are, however, ways of dealing with challenges that can help or hinder us in getting on with life.

A psychologist called Sonja Lyubomirsky has developed the "Happiness Pie" from her research in this area. In it she summarises what is known about what helps people to be happy. It's counterintuitive to the way in which many of us live our lives and make our decisions but it's also rather cheering I think. It goes as follows.

Genetics

About half of our happiness is determined by our genes. This has been shown through twin studies. Identical twins are irresistible to psychologists in trying to resolve "nature/nurture" questions: even with happiness.

Fraternal twins show varying levels of happiness, as you would expect between people, and so do identical twins. But the variation between identical twins is about half that measured in fraternal twins. This genetic element gives us a base line "set point" of happiness, to which we are likely to return pretty much regardless of what happens to us in life.

Circumstances

Our circumstances also affect how happy we feel. This is the interesting part though, as most of us overestimate how important they are in determining our happiness. As a result, we tend to put a lot of energy into what to do about our circumstances. We move house, or get married, or take a new job, or have children. Or we buy things, or re-do the kitchen (again).

Of course, these things, and the negatively perceived circumstances such as bereavement and divorce *do* affect us, particularly in the months or maybe years after they occur. Many of them give our lives meaning, which is not always the same thing as being happy.

Sonja found that they only account for about 10% of our happiness in the longer term. We are very adaptable as humans. We will generally get used to new circumstances after a couple of years or so. It is not that you forget them or stop being pleased or unhappy about them, but people have remarkable capacity to rebuild their lives within the new circumstances. This is even the case when those circumstances are traumatic. This doesn't mean life goes back to what it was. Or that you are not forever altered by some events. But – in most cases – life goes on. Often in ways you may never have imagined.

A great example of this is emerging evidence from Iceland that, following the catastrophic collapse of their economy in 2008, people were depressed. Unemployment rose dramatically. Lifestyles had to alter. However, many people, a couple of years on, have found that their spirits have bounced back. Those still wrestling with very high levels of personal debt are struggling. But it seems that most other people feel they have survived some kind of nightmare together and come through it. Anecdotal evidence from creative businesses here in Nottingham (part of a joint research project with Reykjavik University) indicate that independent and energetic small businesses are now filling the boarded up space left by the high street stores that disappeared. People adapt to the circumstances.

Our interpretation of events

The other 40% of our happiness has been shown to be accounted for *by the way in which we interpret events*. In other words it is our thinking and judgements about events rather than the events themselves that affect our emotional state most of all.

The reason I find this cheering is that our outlook on events can be changed. Our brains are nothing like as fixed in adulthood as was previously thought. This means that old habits of thinking can be changed. It's not necessarily easy. It can require the same amount of effort, support and practice that learning a musical instrument or getting fit might require – but it IS possible.

Strengthening a realistically positive mindset can give us the ability to bounce back from setbacks much more effectively than being defeatist about them. It should be noted that sometimes the most appropriate action to take is to accept defeat. However, it is more about choosing to hit the eject button in a more considered and optimistic way that then means we can move on rather than just throwing in the towel when the going gets tough.

We build up our habits of thinking throughout our lives. The way we are taught, our childhood experiences, the models we are given by the influential adults in our lives, our genes, our friendships, the events we encounter: all of these combine to create habitual ways of interpreting what's going on for us whether we are aware of it or not. These habits can become so familiar that we take them for granted and accept them as the truth of a situation. For example,

"I knew I wouldn't get that promotion, I never have any luck."

"I'm dreading doing that presentation to the Board, they're going to give me a real grilling on my department's results."

"She doesn't like me – so I can't do anything right in her eyes."

"Just keep thinking positive and you'll get well"

These thoughts and many millions like them will flit through our minds every day. Your own particular brand of habit may differ from these. Some habits are more helpful than others, but they all influence the way in which we look for evidence to support them. The habits then get stronger. Every time you don't get a promotion, or don't get a parking space, or get ignored by someone, may then confirm in your mind that you are not a lucky person, or someone else doesn't like you. Any time something happens that reinforces that view, you will notice it. Small things and big things can trigger these automatic interpretations, and you are probably rarely aware of them.

One small common example that I have observed is whether people believe that others are rude on public transport or not. Usually it is possible to find examples of inconsiderate behaviour and also to find examples of kind and thoughtful behaviour. You are likely to notice and remember examples that support your beliefs either way. It is entirely possible that two people could do the same bus journey and one goes home to say how rude the young people of today are, whilst another reports how pleasant it was to see a young person helping a parent on with a pram. Probably both things are true, from different incidents. Our necessarily selective attention keeps reinforcing our interpretations of the world. We would go mad if it didn't in some ways as you cannot pay attention to everything – but it can sometimes be valuable to challenge our habitual interpretations.

Psychologists (who like a bit of jargon) describe some of what goes on here as an "attribution error". This means when something happens we cast around for an explanation and will usually decide that something or someone is the cause (and is to blame). An attribution error is made when we've given the wrong cause to the event. Blaming an unwelcome outcome on being an "unlucky" person can make you feel unhappy (it's a description that implies you have no control over anything so will feel stressful). But it is unlikely to be based on real evidence (stuff seems to happen more to some people than others but I don't think it's a lasting and inherent human quality to be lucky or not). *How* you interpret or label events is the key thing.

What this means and how it is good news

Old dogs

What is becoming clear from the fast-moving field of neuroscience is the great news that our brains are not fixed into hard-wired patterns even when we are adults (see books such as *The Brain that Changes Itself* by Norman Doidge). It might not necessarily be easy but we can (and do) change the way in which our brains work with every new skill or habit, whether those are mental or physical. It is possible to teach old dogs new tricks. Although the old dog really needs to believe it is possible, otherwise he or she is unlikely to put much effort or persistence into learning the new trick.

This means that, whatever it might be, if you are prepared to put some effort into practising, you can change the way your brain works. This is how new skills, habits and behaviours can be picked up. And this includes optimism.

I find this enormously exciting and motivating, especially as I reach middle age myself. It's not too late to learn many things, if I want to.

Notice I do not say that it's not too late for anything. Again, I come back to resisting denial of reality dressed up as positive thinking. It *is* too late for me to be an Olympic ice dancer, or an international footballer, however much I might want to be those things (although it might be considered a little strange that these ambitions didn't occur to me until my mid forties). And some other things might be possible but I don't want them enough to devote every waking minute to working at them. Even if I did, if it is a question of being the best person in the world at something, the realistic chances are probably slim.

In short – you can learn more helpful thinking strategies to lead you to be able to deal with what life throws at you more successfully, but you can't win *The X Factor* (or anything else) just by wanting it, thinking positive and denying the reality that is involved.

What might stop us from wanting to become more optimistic?

The fact that we can still change the way our brains are wired, even into adulthood, means that it is a realistic goal to learn to be more optimistic. So why wouldn't we all rush off to do so?

Braced for the worst

For a long time, I personally held a philosophy that went something like this:

If I imagine the worst outcome to the situation I am about to go into, then anything that happens that isn't as bad as I imagine will be a bonus (and therefore I will enjoy and appreciate it more).

It was exhausting. Every time something went well I had a sense of getting away with it this time but what about next time? If it went badly, it was only confirming my expectations. If someone had said to me "You can learn to be more optimistic" I would have been sceptical (imagine the worst...).

Life was full of "*What ifs*" this or that happened, bracing myself for something that usually never occurred.

Through my psychology and coaching work, I realise this is quite a common philosophy, or at least variations of it are common. It's not just me.

Hard work (and maybe a bit daunting)

Changing habits, whether of thinking or doing, is hard work. This is true of any other beneficial habits: a healthy diet, or taking more exercise, for example. Even when the need to change these habits is screaming at us, it doesn't mean that the obvious benefits are enough for us to be successful in doing so.

We need to recognise the strength of the assumptions we hold that keep old, less helpful habits in place, as well as the strength of the fears that may accompany changing them. Be gentle with yourself. Acknowledge that there can be real underlying fears about changing, even when the change would be for the better and we want to do it. These fears are often deeply founded and very powerful, even if flawed. Exposed to a dose of fresh air and reality, they can sometimes seem slightly ridiculous.

Will no one like me any more if I'm fit, optimistic, confident? Will I no longer be the self-effacing humble person I quietly pride myself on? Am I comfortable in my role as "victim" to circumstances rather than optimistically bouncing back when something I don't like happens?

There are lots of ways to identify these fears and support the changes that people want to put in place. Some cognitive behavioural therapy can help, and another useful approach is outlined by Robert Kegan and Lisa Laskow Lahey in their book, *Immunity to Change*.

For me, delving into all this in some detail over the years has led me to realise I could safely change the way I was thinking and that this would lead to much more interesting, enjoyable, energising and productive times. The key is recognising that it takes time, commitment and support to turn our thinking habits around.

Characteristics of pessimists and optimists

"Life inflicts the same setbacks and tragedies on the optimist as on the pessimist, but the optimist weathers them better."
—Martin Seligman

One of the original psychologists to make a mark in this area is Martin Seligman, author of *Learned Helplessness*, *Learned Optimism* and most recently, *Flourish*. By his work, an optimist is absolutely NOT someone who blindly believes good things will happen without any evidence. He describes the defining characteristics of pessimists and optimists as follows:

Pessimists tend to believe bad events will last a long time, will undermine everything they do, and are their fault.

Optimists tend to believe bad events are temporary setbacks, with causes associated with one event at a time rather than part of a pattern of defeat. They believe circumstances, bad luck or other people were responsible for the bad event.

Similarly, the way pessimists and optimists view good events is different too. Vice versa in fact.

Pessimists tend to believe that good events are temporary strokes of good luck. Circumstances, good luck or other people were responsible for the good event.

Optimists tend to believe that they are at least partially responsible for good events. The events may have required hard work to bring about, or practice at a skill, or being proactive to organise an event or nurture the relationships involved in it.

Taking the two psychologists' work together (Lyubomirsky and Seligman), I conclude that this means that pessimists place their faith in circumstances to bring about their happiness or well-being whereas optimists place their faith in themselves to a much greater extent.

In a western society, where advertising and marketing is so powerful (maybe because of our economic models of growth), we are encouraged to believe the pessimist's version. If we change our circumstances by having a new gadget or car or moving to a bigger house or job we are promised that we will feel happier. The short burst of euphoria we probably experience when we get these things persuades us of the truth of that misconception (another instance of a form of attribution error). When it wears off, because we adapt to our new circumstance, we trundle off to find the next change of circumstance that will bring about that happiness fix.

Random accidents of life happen to everyone alike. It is not that optimists don't experience or anticipate bad events. Nor is it that they don't get upset by them. Nor is it that they don't enjoy new circumstances. They just don't rely on them as much as pessimists do for the good times.

The consequences of these two approaches mean that optimists are much less likely to give up in the face of defeat, are less likely to get depressed, tend to have better health, and do better at school and work. There is some evidence that they may even live longer.

That seems to make it worth developing in my mind.

What strategies can help you become more optimistic?

Good but boring news

Learning to change a habit of pessimistic thought takes some awareness and vigilance (spotting the pessimistic thoughts can be tricky in itself sometimes as they are usually so familiar); a lot of practice; support from others; and a commitment to doing it. This is much the same as learning any other new skill or habit: getting fit, learning a language, taking up dancing.

This is kind of good but boring news.

It doesn't sell books or courses if the buyer is looking for a quick and easy fix, any more than diet books telling you about a healthy balanced diet and slow weight loss are likely to sell the same number of books as one that promises rapid change through an interesting and easy rule.

The good bit though is that we are increasingly knowledgeable about what actually works rather than what some guru or other might attractively suggest. Habits change slowly and with some difficulty: pick one at a time, get some support, and try it. If you forget or stop, remember that this is common with new habits – and start again.

Some good habits worth trying

Spot when you are thinking in a way that isn't actually based on any external evidence, however true it might seem at the time. It takes practice to do that and a structured approach to gently challenging that thinking. I am not going to cover the details here but highlight some of the typical issues which can be effectively dealt with. You may wish to take it further and find a suitably qualified cognitive behavioural therapist who can, in many cases, clearly identify unhelpful thinking habits and support change. In cognitive behavioural terms, these are called "thinking errors".

We are subjective beings (of course). We all have a limited view of the world because we can't be everywhere at once to have a truly balanced weighing up of all perspectives on any given situation. But some of the necessary assumptions we make in order to decide what to do next may mean that we:

- **Take a very all or nothing approach** – see everything in pass or fail, good or bad terms. Few things are genuinely like this, much as it might be convenient to label them as such. Arguably, many parts of the media like to label things or people clearly good or bad, no in-between. For example, a presentation you found difficult; a colleague you find hard to get on with; a test you got 60% on rather than the 80% you thought you could have done and your friend got – all of these are likely to be partially successful but very often we'll dismiss them in our minds as total failures. This assessment then makes us *feel* like failures. And then we (rationally) want to avoid the situation in the future.
- **Using words like *never, always, everyone, no one.*** As a parent of teenagers I am very alert to these. *Everyone* else has a later bedtime, more pocket money, is more cool/popular. Things will *never* change; my life will *always* be like this. Adults do it too. These thinking errors are hard to spot, because they seem true. But when you do spot them, gently challenge them. The chances are they're not actually true. It may be things that happen a lot, or that most people do or have various things. It's probably not always and everyone though.

- **Mind-reading and fortune telling.** We all have to interpret what other people might be thinking from what they say or their actions. We might just be wrong though. This doesn't stop people carrying on as if they know exactly what someone else thinks of them or has a particular agenda. In the same way, we often think we know exactly what will happen in a given situation. Sometimes we may be right (which can lead to some satisfying "told you so" moments). But the evidence is that people aren't very good at accurate predictions (at any level). That doesn't stop us acting as if we are great at it ("I know my boss is going to give me a hard time", "I know we're not going to get any orders next week"). Again, spot them and challenge gently.
- **Predicting catastrophes.** This is a particular form of fortune telling. It is characteristic of highly anxious states and is very easy to get drawn into if people around you are doing it too. Again, there is usually limited, if any, evidence that the disaster you are predicting will actually come to pass. Even if things aren't great, it is usually much easier to deal with actual events than it is to deal with the terrifying imagined ones.
- **Dustbin labels.** We do it a lot but it doesn't make us feel good. "I'm hopeless at maths", "I'm not creative", "I'm a dreadful cook" (arguably a particularly British trait? To give dustbin labels I mean, not the cooking. I live in hope that the reputation Britain had for bad food has passed by now.). Some things play to our strengths more than others but this harsh blanket assessment just stops you trying. How about "I find maths difficult so I need to practise a lot or get some extra help" instead. You get the picture.
- **Mindful meditation.** There's more on this in the chapter about a mental break. One of the benefits is that it can

break the cycle of rumination or "over-thinking" which can be linked with depression. Constantly running through *what ifs* as I described earlier is a form of unhelpful rumination. Ten minutes of mindful meditation a day can begin to calm this often unconscious but anxiety-producing process.

- **Remember the good bits of your day.** Even in the worst days, there are likely to be a few things that went well or that you noticed (or could have noticed) as being interesting, beautiful, funny, kind or marvellous. Research by Martin Seligman has shown that writing down three or so things that fall into this category for every day for some weeks can lift mild depression, and enhance the positive outlook of people who wouldn't classify themselves as depressed. It helps to bring about a "glass half full" attitude. I recall an interesting piece written by one of the survivors of the underground bomb attacks in London in July 2005. They recalled the jokes made in the carriage they were trapped in after the blast. Black humour indeed, and in no one's estimation would that count as a good or successful day for those involved. But even in extremis there can be some good bits to notice.

- **Seek help.** We all face circumstances that frighten us or threaten to overwhelm us. If we don't ever experience those, it may mean we're living deep within our comfort zone which may not be in our long term best interests. At the beginning of the chapter we met Bea Hunter. She told me she made a conscious decision to let her husband Mike take the reins of the company when she was feeling overwhelmed and pessimistic – and to trust him. With a smile, she said she didn't find this easy. But the level of help and support they provide for each other (as well as being good at asking for help of other people too) is one of the key aspects to their continued entrepreneurial journey.

As Helen Keller said, "Optimism is the faith that leads to achievement. Nothing can be done without hope and confidence."
She became one of the world's great movers and shakers as a deaf-blind woman in the early twentieth century. That can't have been easy. Just shows what optimism can lead to.

CHAPTER ONE – IN BRIEF

- It is possible to learn to be more optimistic and deal with setbacks more constructively.
- Our circumstances are less important than our outlook in how happy we feel.
- It takes some hard work, practice and support to change our interpretation of events, but it can be done.

LEARN MORE

- *Learned Optimism and Flourish* by Martin Seligman. American psychologist Martin Seligman is seen as the founder of the positive psychology movement. A good place to start if you are interested in finding out more. *Flourish* is his most recent book.
- *The How of Happiness* by Sonja Lyubomirsky – another influential American professor of psychology, Sonja's book is accessible, practical and grounded in research findings.
- *Action for Happiness*, www.actionforhappiness.org. This British movement, founded in 2010 by Richard Layard, Geoff Mulgan and Anthony Seldon has no religious, political or commercial affiliations and its aim is to bring people together to create a happier society. The web site has lots more information.
- *The Feeling Good Handbook* by David Burns, or *Cognitive Behavioural Therapy for Dummies* by Rob Willson and Rhena Branch – or search for a self help book that appeals to you written by a qualified cognitive behavioural therapist for more on thinking errors and ways to challenge them.

You might also be able to access on line or face to face cognitive behavioural therapy through your doctor.

A complete list of references can be found at the end of the book.

CHAPTER 2

STRESS: HOW TO DEAL WITH THE LAST STRAW

*In 2008/09 an estimated 415 000 people in Great Britain, who worked in the previous year, believed that they were suffering from **stress, depression or anxiety** caused or made worse by their current or past work. This equates to 1400 per 100 000 people (1.4%) who worked in the last 12 months in Great Britain.*

*An estimated 11.4 million working days (full-day equivalent) were lost in 2008/09 through self-reported **stress, depression or anxiety** caused or made worse by work. On average, each person suffering took an estimated 27.5 days off in that 12 month period.*

(Results from the Labour Force Survey 2008/9)

Who's most likely to be stressed at work?

Anyone can suffer from stress. But the profile of the person most likely to report feeling stressed at work is as follows:

....

Mr or Ms Stressed
- Divorced/separated or widowed
- 41-50 years old
- Full-time employee

- Educated to degree level
- Above average salary (at least £20,000)
- Professional or managerial position

(from Health and Safety Executive (HSE) contract research report 311/2000)

*It should be noted this is a correlation not a causal relationship – having these characteristics does not necessarily mean you will become stressed – it's just that more people who have these are also feeling stressed.

....

Many of the people I know and/or coach tick at least four or five of those boxes, and are therefore more likely to report feeling stressed than other working groups. Stress can be a very real problem. And these figures relate to those who are in work. If you are out of work, the stress levels can be even higher.

What are we talking about?

Stress ...

... is the adverse reaction people have to excessive pressures or other types of demand placed on them at work. (HSE)
... results from an imbalance between demands and resources. (Lazarus and Folkman, 1984)
... a situation where demands on a person exceed that person's resources or ability to cope. (HSE, 2004)
... can only be sensibly defined as a perceptual phenomenon arising from a comparison between the demand on the person and his or her ability to cope. An imbalance in this mechanism, when coping is important, gives rise to the experience of stress, and to the stress response. (T. Cox, 1978)
... is an invitation to change something. (I don't know who said that first ... but it makes you think.)

There has been a great deal of research in the field of stress and this is not the place to go through it all in detail. However, it is important to base what to do on a real understanding of what is going on. What follows is the way I explain what stress is, which I have found to be useful in practice with individual clients. It is drawn mainly from the research done for the Health and Safety Executive (HSE) over many years, much of which was led by Professor Tom Cox.

Taking an organisational approach (which I am not going into in this book) is also vital if stress is to be prevented and managed in the workplace. The HSE website is a good starting point.

A model of stress

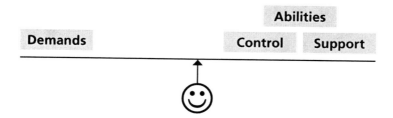

The diagram above is a simple way of summarising the research. It should be noted that it is our *perception* of this balance that is important.

In other words, an unpleasant (and indeed possibly overwhelming) stress response can follow if we don't *think* that the demands we face can be met by a combination of our own abilities, our control over the situation and the amount of support we can call on.

This can go either way too – it may be that the demands aren't high enough (for example, in a monotonous job where you are bored) and the imbalance is just as stressful as when those demands are considered to be far too high.

And then what happens?

If we judge that we don't have the ability, control and support to meet the demands (and our judgement is key in this – someone else in a similar situation may find it more or less stressful than we do), we are likely to experience some or all of the following. It's not fun.

....

When the last straw is added...

Emotional symptoms
- Negative or depressive feeling
- Disappointment with yourself
- Increased emotional reactions – more tearful or sensitive or aggressive
- Loneliness, withdrawn
- Loss of motivation commitment and confidence
- Mood swings (not behavioural)

Mental
- Confusion, indecision
- Can't concentrate
- Poor memory

Changes from your normal behaviour
- Changes in eating habits
- Increased smoking, drinking or drug taking 'to cope'
- Mood swings affecting your behaviour
- Changes in sleep patterns
- Twitchy, nervous behaviour
- Changes in attendance such as arriving later or taking more time off

(from HSE website)

....

What can you do if the last straw is added for you?

From this explanation of stress, it is easy to see that it is possible for anyone to experience it. People vary widely in their judgements and interpretations of how many, and what type, of demands they can cope with. We are all different. The last straw will take very different forms for different people, and even at different times in one person's life. Some fortunate people may never experience a last straw (which can lead them to assuming that stress doesn't exist).

None of us can be certain that we will never be in a situation where we feel that balance tip though – and when it does tip, it can feel overwhelming and downright frightening.

If it does tip...

The strategy to take is to work towards restoring that balance. Let's look at each element in turn, starting with support as I think it is the most important one once you are feeling stressed.

Support

Asking for help can be one of the most difficult things to do, especially if you are feeling overwhelmed and panicked, and your confidence is at a low point. It is known that these feelings are, counterproductively, likely to make you withdraw from other people. However, this is the time where asking for help is the most effective thing to do.

- **If you are feeling depressed or even suicidal** – seek help from your GP or a help line such as the Samaritans (confidential emotional support) or organisation such as Cruse (bereavement care) or Relate (for relationship problems), or maybe your organisation has a counselling or emergency help service. These are usually accessible in confidence. Don't be tempted to wait until things feel unbearable before you do this.

- **Friends or family** can be very valuable sources of support. You will have an idea of which ones are the best listeners, and sometimes you can find unexpected people prove to be particularly good in a crisis. Asking for someone to listen or admitting to someone that you are not coping can seem like a massive deal – but very often, that is a perception rather than reality. If you can find the courage (and it really does take some nerve when you are feeling vulnerable) to contact a friend, colleague or even a stranger and ask directly for help or a listening ear, the chances are that person will be only too willing to support you. You probably would be if it was *them* asking *you* (most people feel flattered at some level to be chosen as a confidant).

- **If the stress has particular causes,** then seeking support to address those is vital if anything is to change. It may be that you need some extra help with a particular project. Maybe you have a very difficult client and need some back up. Maybe the timescales you are being asked to work to are impossibly tight. Or maybe all the domestic chores are falling to you on top of your work.

So often, I come across people for whom asking directly for help in these situations is not on their radar. The more stressed they get, the less likely it seems that they will even think of asking for help. It can seem very obvious from the outside. But once someone is in that stressed out place they often can't see what, or who, could help.

....

The promising young manager

Many years ago, I met a stressed and uncharacteristically tearful young manager who had just turned down a promotion. At a separate and unconnected meeting, his manager happened to mention that they couldn't understand why this rising star employee had refused their offer.

Eventually, it all transpired that his wife was expecting a baby later in the year and he didn't want to be away or extra busy when that happened. The new job was going to involve a time consuming project involving a lot of travel. It had just not occurred to him to ask whether the organisation could help him balance these things. He was working on an assumption that his private life was his own problem to manage out of sight of his work. He was worrying himself sick about it.

The relief all round once the situation was revealed was tangible. Conversations ensued that led to adjusting responsibilities and timing of the project so that he could be involved as well as staying locally based for the weeks around the birth. His career was far from ruined by this. The organisation kept him as they very much wanted to.

And his stress levels rapidly went down.

....

Demands

Demands have a way of building up and you may enthusiastically (or not) say yes to a whole variety of requests.

Managing demands in the longer term requires clarity about when to say yes and when to say no.

Once submerged under an overwhelming pile of demands though, it can be very difficult to see the wood for the trees and it can seem as if everything is an urgent priority.

You may well need some help to work out how to deal with the demands once they feel like this. You may need to consult your manager, clients or family to work out the answers to these sorts of difficult questions:

- Can the demands you face be reduced?
- Can someone else take on some of them (delegate)?
- Can some of them be re-scheduled (do they *have* to be done right now)?
- Can you reduce the standard of what needs to be done without compromising the end result? (That might be particularly relevant if you have perfectionist tendencies)
- Is there a more efficient way of dealing with the demands?
- Are you clear about what you are aiming to achieve and what outcomes are necessary or desirable?
- If you can't meet all of the demands, it is usually better to communicate that this is the case. If you keep quiet, you risk missing deadlines and aggravating the situation. If I am ever on the receiving end of such a situation, I would much rather be kept informed and try to work with that person or organisation to reach a compromise than be strung along. The most tangible example recently for me was having a house extension built by a firm that went bust half way through the job. The broken promises and lack of communication about delivery deadlines were arguably the most difficult aspect to deal with. Once we knew what was going on, we could work with it more constructively and

get to completion (albeit six months late – but it should be noted the world didn't end as a result).

Abilities

There may be things you need to learn to be able to complete particular tasks. Being stretched beyond our comfort zone is usually a good thing as it means we are learning and building up our skills and experience, but if it feels as if you are too far out of your depth, it can be very stressful.

- **How can you identify what gaps there might be in your understanding or skills?** It might be best to get some help (again, the support can be a first step in being able to see these things more clearly) to work this out. Often, it is easy to make blanket assessments of your (in)ability to do various things – "I can't do it". When this is explored a bit more closely, it can be more useful to identify which parts of a task you are happy with and which parts you might need to learn more about. Try to pinpoint specific areas where you could ask for more explanation, or consciously set out to learn more about. It's easier to ask for the right training or explanation once you have broken a seemingly insurmountable task down into smaller components.
- **Remember your strengths.** When people are stressed, they can have a tendency to focus on all the things they think they can't do very well, and to dismiss all those qualities and skills that they do have. As Alex Linley, respected psychologist and expert on identifying and using strengths, says, "none of us is equipped with what it takes to be brilliant at everything … the secret to success lies in making the best of what we have and aligning it effectively to what we want to achieve."

Control

Control is an odd concept really. Clearly there are very many things that we don't have within our control. Some people can spend a huge amount of energy trying to achieve an elusive level of control over some of those things. Certain times in our lives can feel stressful because our sense of control has diminished: new parenthood, for example, or if we fall ill. Redundancy programmes often have the same effect.

In terms of stress, it is the perception of control as much as the *actual* control that can make a difference. *Feeling* out of control in an unwelcome way is what is likely to precipitate a stress response. Acceptance is a related concept that is also very important. There is some truth to the somewhat over-quoted serenity prayer: *Grant me the serenity to accept the things I cannot change, courage to change the things I can, and wisdom to know the difference.*

- **Take some time to write down** what is within your control and what isn't. In a stressed state, it may well feel as if nothing is. However, some things almost certainly are, even if it amounts to small things like choosing what you eat, or whether to go out for a walk.

  Ellen Langer, an American psychologist, has studied this area in some depth. She carried out a well known study where elderly residents in a care home were given houseplants to care for. Or at least some of them were, while others were given plants but they were watered and cared for by the staff. The results were a real eye-opener. Ellen writes, "A year and a half later, not only were these people [the former group] more cheerful, active, and alert than [the latter group], but many more of them were still alive."

However overwhelming your sense of being out of control might be, try to pin down and hold on to those elements of life and work, however small, that you *can* do something about.

- **Focus** on those things, however trivial they might seem. One thing at a time.
- **Mindfulness** and some kinds of therapy can help to bring a healthy acceptance of situations that you can't alter. This is not the same as giving up. But it can acknowledge a change in your circumstances that may have been unwelcome and create the opportunity to move on from it. It's not necessarily easy and doesn't happen overnight (and often needs some support from others) – but it can happen. I will return to the subject of mindfulness in chapter four where we explore ways of taking mental breaks.

In a large landscape of lack of control, the tiny things can make a difference. This is why people will persist in small rituals and acts even in the most difficult of circumstances.

....

The case of Viktor Frankl

Viktor Frankl's book *Man's Search for Meaning* is probably one of most inspiring and influential reflections on this topic. A psychiatrist held in four different Nazi concentration camps during the war, he describes in vivid detail many of his experiences. At the end of one especially bad day (in the sixth winter of the war), the inmates were encouraged by a rather unusual block warden who showed real signs of humanity to talk about what was on their minds. Viktor was elected by the warden to talk to the others. He writes:

"God knows, I was not in the mood to give psychological explanations or to preach any sermons ... I was cold and hungry, irritable and tired ... but I had to make the effort and use of this unique opportunity.

I said that each of us had to ask himself what irreplaceable losses he had suffered up till then. I speculated that for most of them these losses had really been few. Whoever was still alive had reason for hope. Health, family, happiness, professional abilities, fortune, position in society – all these were things that could be achieved again or restored."

So it proved for Viktor himself. He went on to have a long productive life, dying of old age in 1997 and leaving a huge professional legacy as well as a child, wife and grandchildren.

What he points out in many appalling circumstances throughout the book, is that the perception of control – however slim – feeds hope. He argues, forcefully and convincingly, that hope was – is – essential to survival.

....

And a note on taking care of yourself

The next chapter will go into some more depth about ways to well-being. It is worth noting here that people who are experiencing high stress levels often put their own needs quite low on the agenda. If the last straw has hit you, it may be that you are not eating well, sleeping well, taking much exercise or time off. You may be drinking more or your immunity to illness may be lower. You may feel lonely.

This book aims to address many of the interconnected areas that I believe help us to maintain a good position to deal with (and even enjoy) the demands we face.

If a combination of difficult demands has hit you in recent times, and you feel that your resources to deal with them are depleted, do give yourself a break: literally or metaphorically. Treat yourself with some gentleness at a time when often the opposite happens and we can give ourselves a harder and harder time, beating ourselves up for perceived failures. Be kind to yourself.

Ask for, and accept, help.

Re-build your energy and resources.

It's a cliché, but whatever your last straw is, *this too will pass.*

CHAPTER TWO – IN BRIEF

- Stress can happen to anyone.
- It is important to take an organisational and individual approach when dealing with work-related stress.
- Tackling demands, support, abilities and control, and your perception of these, can alleviate stress related feelings. I would argue that seeking appropriate support is the best first step, and the rest can lead from that.

LEARN MORE

- *The Compassionate Mind* by Paul Gilbert – a wise book on being kind to yourself and others to foster courage and resilience.
- *First Things First* by Stephen Covey, A. Roger Merrill and Rebecca R. Merrill – there are many books available on time management but this has helped some clients of mine with a practical view of how to prioritise when faced with many competing demands.
- *Preventing Stress in Organizations: How to Develop Positive Managers* by Emma Donaldson-Feilder, Rachel Lewis and Joanna Yarker – for a good introduction to organisational approaches to stress.
- *Counterclockwise* by Ellen Langer – a BBC series was based on this book (called *The Young Ones*, originally broadcast in December 2010). Very interesting read in my view.

A complete list of references can be found at the end of the book.

CHAPTER 3

IN THE EYE OF THE STORM: DEALING WITH CHANGE AND UNCERTAINTY

Patrick Markham was, until recently, the head of a big department in the UK at a global telecommunications company. He had worked hard for many years to reach this position, and as a senior manager now had a responsible and rewarding job, with 250 staff reporting to him.

Then the company decided to close the operation where he worked. Patrick, and many others, moved to a brand new site fifty miles away. It meant more commuting but was manageable. Then, unexpectedly, the company announced that it was closing that site too.

A spokesman for the company was reported as saying that they recognised it was a difficult time but were having to increase efficiency and lower the cost base to deliver solutions designed to meet global customers' needs.

A very difficult business decision.

One that Patrick and the rest of the senior management team knew about for several weeks before most of the workforce but, although they tried, were unable to influence. They had still hoped there could be a different outcome, for business reasons quite aside from their own personal situation. When it became definite, Patrick had to tell staff this was going to happen, even though he had encouraged many of them to move to the new site only the previous year.

Over the best part of a year, he was involved in supporting others and closing the site, handing over on-going projects and knowledge to other parts of the company, and then being one of the last to leave - effectively being the one to turn out the lights as he left.

He was made redundant at the end of September 2010. I met him for a coffee and a chat about six months on, to talk about his experiences.

"I was warned about how this would be. Whilst still at work, I was focussed on the needs of the team and my responsibilities. I found it easier to do that than stare at my own blank piece of paper. But then the end date comes and you reach a cliff yourself."

He was offered the opportunity with considerable financial incentive to move abroad. But with family and friends in the UK, including children at school, he didn't want to uproot this far. He also felt that, whilst he still respected the company, his trust that they could look after individual employees in the current economic environment had been eroded by his experiences.

"By not taking an overseas job, to some extent I chose to jump off that cliff into uncertainty. It did make us think when a few weeks later a colleague who had re-located to the Silicon Valley sent us pictures of his big house and swimming pool. Of course there was that moment of 'That could have been us'"

But he and his wife knew why it wasn't in their heart of hearts. He said, "I have to remind myself I chose not to do that for the right reasons so don't panic."

Patrick has decided (through careful consideration with extensive outplacement support in his months before redundancy) to use this situation to shift career focus if possible.

He says, "With all due respect to the telecommunications industry, at the end of the day, it is still widgets (high quality ones at that). I want to do something more aligned to my growing interest in social enterprise – the ideal for me would be working for one of the big charities such as Oxfam."

He has been working in a management role at a local social enterprise and learning a lot about this field (including making successful bids for grant funding) since being made redundant, in addition to taking on new voluntary roles such as school governor. But he knows that it is unsustainable for him to work on a voluntary basis for very long.

Patrick has taken a disciplined approach to managing his time over the past six months. He programmes in monthly planning and reviewing time and is methodical about continuing to develop good networks, structure his time and to do regular exercise. But he is aware that this is getting harder as time goes on.

"It takes more emotional energy to keep self motivated, rather than simply respond to the demands and requirements of others. It is more important than ever, but you need more resilience as time goes on too.

"I am conscious that I am feeling more vulnerable too. Small things going wrong seem bigger than they would have done before. And – I don't know if it's a coincidence – I was hospitalised recently with a serious infection which came from nowhere. I've never experienced anything like that before. I do wonder if my immune system is not what it usually is.

"The loneliness is an issue too. Whilst I belong to many groups socially, and have family and friends, I miss the day to day connection with people that work brought. There's lots of space now where there was none. It's good and bad."

The benefits of more family time were not unexpected but an important factor in the decision not to move abroad.

Less expected benefits include becoming more aware of the environment where he lives and local issues that he was never conscious of when working long hours. For example, a nearby mental health drop in centre is threatened with closure and he has become involved with supporting the staff and campaigners fighting for its existence. He'd never noticed it was there before.

It is highly unlikely that someone of Patrick's calibre is going to be in this situation for very long. Whilst we were talking, his phone rang with a request for him to come to an interview. But in some ways, as he says, it can be difficult that others can't quite believe this is happening to him.

"They say to me 'of course it'll be ok, you've got great experience and CV, and you're really good.' These things are true, but there starts to be a feeling of stigma about it. I'm much more aware of how illusory the security is that most of us take for granted; how near to the surface that lack of security might be in other people and you would never guess."

In their different ways, big global business, the publicly funded and the charitable sectors – and Patrick – are in the eye of the storm.

Plus ça change, plus c'est la même chose

The more things change, the more they stay the same
– Jean-Baptiste Alphonse Karr, 1849

Every generation has probably thought that they are facing unprecedented change. Maybe it is part of the human condition that we think that and maybe it is true; each generation does face its own turmoil and progress. Without it, the world would be caught in some unbearable kind of Groundhog Day.

In hindsight, we weave a narrative around events, whether personal or shared, that seems to give them a beginning, middle and end. It may even give them a purpose or meaning if we're lucky. When we are in the thick of it though, it can be very hard to make sense of what's going on or to work out what the best course of action would be.

I often wonder what it must have been like for my grandparents who were young parents at the outbreak of the second world war (younger than I am now). One grandfather died during the war, the other three grandparents survived. It wasn't an unusual set of circumstances for families around the world, and we could be considered to have got off lightly compared with millions less fortunate.

My generation looks back now, knowing the ultimate outcome of the war, how long it lasted and that it was worth hanging in there in the end. But the world population at the time didn't know any of that. Imagine how great the uncertainty was faced by Londoners in the blitz in the depth of the winter in 1940/41, to take just one of many examples from across the world.

In a similar way, Patrick may look back on this period of time in the future and be able to see where it led him and how he both managed and, hopefully, gained from the situation. It will become a coherent story.

Right now, however, he faces an unpredictable future.

Actually, though, an unpredictable future is a constant for all of us; whether we choose to think of it that way or not.

Beginnings, middles and ends

Having a model of what might be going on can be a reassuring way of explaining how we might be feeling and acting at these times. This is a model that I personally have found helpful and many of the people I coach have too.

William Bridges and transition

William Bridges is a consultant and author who has written extensively on the subject of transition, both from a personal perspective and from the view of an organisation. I find his three stages a very useful framework for thinking about our psychological reaction to change.

1. **Endings** – what it says on the tin. It may be the end of a job, relationship, life – or something less obvious like the end of an identity (as a child-free adult when you become a parent for instance). Sometimes these endings have fanfares (and leaving parties), and sometimes they are less easily recognised.

2. **Middles (or the "neutral" zone)** – this is the eye of the storm. Uncomfortable and potentially the most creative stage, it is a time of feeling empty or confused, where neither the old ways of doing things or viewing the world nor new ways seem to work properly. As Bridges describes it "It is a phase when you've let go of one trapeze with the faith that the new trapeze is on its way. In the meantime, there is nothing to hold on to". I call this "camping". More on that soon.

3. **New beginnings** – endings and beginnings are what the greetings card industry is built on. Good luck with the new house/job/child/marriage and off you go. It is often less clear and more ambivalent than you might think though. Sometimes it is more to do with something "feeling right" than the external pointers to change. It can take some trial and error, and adjustment, before a new beginning really feels as if it fits.

These stages don't necessarily follow neatly in order. You may find yourself floundering around a bit with a few false starts and new understandings of what was involved in the endings. And the neutral zone is by definition a period of floundering in some ways.

(taken from William Bridges *Transitions: making sense of life's changes*)

....

Camping

I tend to think of the neutral zone as camping. I am going to focus on this stage of transition because it is often the most difficult and the most rewarding at the same time. It is also often the one that people want to rush through to nail a new beginning at all costs.

At this point, nothing seems like you thought it was, or as you had hoped it would be. Something has ended and left you high and dry one way or another. Even when this is a welcome change that you initiated (moving house or job, for example, or retiring), it can still, often unexpectedly, leave you reeling in the uncertainty that accompanies the end of an era.

This can engender an urgency to get something new in place as quickly as possible. The re-bound relationship is the classic example of that. For Patrick, it might have taken the form of moving to the States. It might not be the wrong thing to do. But it is, ironically, risky in its illusion of safety and security.

As Bridges says, and I can testify to, this period of time can be immensely valuable. It's a time when you can get to know yourself better, experiment with new ideas, experience more extremes of emotion, have some fun and let go of old mindsets that may not be serving you very well any more. It can be a time when you feel more alive than ever before.

It is, however, very important to take care of yourself whilst all this is going on or it can be overwhelming.

That's why I think of it as camping. When a natural disaster hits, the world responds by providing first aid, food, water, blankets and tents in the first instance. This buys time and temporary shelter whilst we work out what has gone on and how we're going to deal with it. In the same way that it would be foolish to rush into building a new tower block to provide immediate relief in an earthquake zone, it can be equally foolish to leap at some permanent solution in our own turbulent situations. However tempting that might be.

Bridges' sound advice includes:

- Accept that feelings of confusion, fear and vulnerability are normal at this stage.
- Accept that this takes time. Some days will be better than others. Some days may seem as if they are leading nowhere, or are a step backwards. Be patient.

And I think this is a good time to introduce the Five Ways to Well-being.

The Five Ways to Well-being

The five ways to well-being are a straightforward way to remember the key things that enhance our well-being; that is, whether we are feeling good and functioning well. It may not be quite the same thing as feeling happy in the moment, although it can encompass that.

These five actions are taken from the Foresight project Mental Capital and Well-being published in October 2008. The project commissioned the centre for well-being at nef (the new economics foundation) to develop 'five ways to well-being': a set of evidence-based actions to improve personal well-being.

That rather dry sentence means something very exciting that I feel needs shouting from the rooftops.

The results of this work are simple and succinct. **It gives us five easy to remember and apply principles that work.** If you remember nothing else, remember these. They'll help you flourish.

In the context of change and uncertainty, and camping, these will help you gather your psychological resources in order to move on (when you're ready). Think of them as your tent and blankets.

....

The Five Ways to Well-being

1. **Connect** with the people around you. With family, friends, colleagues and neighbours. At home, work, school or in your local community. Think of these as the cornerstones of your life and invest time in developing them. Building these connections will support and enrich you every day.
2. **Be active** – go for a walk or a run. Step outside. Cycle. Play a game. Garden. Dance. Exercising makes you feel good. Most importantly, discover a physical activity you enjoy; one that suits your level of mobility and fitness.
3. **Take notice** – Be curious. Catch sight of the beautiful. Remark on the unusual. Notice the changing seasons. Savour the moment, whether you are on a train, eating lunch or talking to friends. Be aware of the world around you and what you are feeling. Reflecting on your experiences will help you appreciate what matters to you.
4. **Keep learning** – Try something new. Rediscover an old interest. Sign up for that course. Take on a different

responsibility at work. Fix a bike. Learn to play an instrument or how to cook your favourite food. Set a challenge you will enjoy achieving. Learning new things will make you more confident, as well as being fun to do.

5. **Give** – Do something nice for a friend, or a stranger. Thank someone. Smile. Volunteer your time. Join a community group. Look out, as well as in. Seeing yourself, and your happiness, linked to the wider community can be incredibly rewarding and will create connections with the people around you.

(© nef , the new economics foundation – an independent think and do tank. You can find out more about their work on www.neweconomicsfoundation.org)

....

These things, undertaken consistently, can start to bring benefits very quickly. Maintain them for longer and you will boost your reserves of energy and hope. This will stand you in good stead for navigating your way out of the storm you are currently experiencing.

Making decisions

There can be real pressure, from ourselves as well as others, to make decisions at any time in our lives, but especially when there is a lot of uncertainty. It is easy to feel like there is too much choice in some ways. Choice has been something of a pursuit in itself in many societies recently. It is not necessarily a bad thing, but it sometimes doesn't bring the satisfaction that we (and politicians) think it might.

Barry Schwartz, in his book *The Paradox of Choice: Why more is less* argues that the level of choice we are faced with in a modern western society is actually paralysing and stressful.

For example, if you type "mobile phones" into the UK Amazon web site, it comes up with nearly a million results. This is on an item that didn't even exist for most of us much longer than a decade ago.

If you are trying to make choices about your future when you are in the midst of turmoil of one sort or another, it can seem as if there are endless possible paths. Each has consequences that we can only guess at, and each has some barriers to be overcome too. It can be exhausting.

....

Are you a maximiser or a satisficer?

For **maximisers,** only the best will do. They want to be sure that they got the best product or deal that was available. They will shop around; weigh up options; read reviews: because you cannot choose the best unless you know what all the alternatives are.

Satisficers, on the other hand, settle for something that is good enough and don't worry that there might be something better out there. They usually have criteria for what they are looking for and once those criteria are met, they stop looking for further choices.

Isn't satisficing settling for second best? As Schwartz says "the difference between the two is that the satisficer is content with the merely excellent as opposed to the absolute best".

Maximising can be painful. If you do not (or cannot) know all the information, maximisers will continue to keep trying to make a well-informed decision on the basis of speculation rather than fact. This is potentially a no-win choice. The agonies that school or health care choice can bring illustrate this pain very well.

Post decision regret

Maximisers are likely to have much more debilitating regret which even includes anticipated regret ie. before they have even made a decision they are thinking about how much they might regret the things they didn't choose. That really is being spoiled for choice. I've seen people do it with pudding menus.

Adaptation

We all get used to things, but we often forget that when we are faced with a new choice. The novelty wears off most things. Some people get hooked on that novelty rush, whether with things or people. It's a form of maximising – there may be a better thing, job, friend or partner out there somewhere.

(taken from Barry Schwartz *The Paradox of Choice*)

....

How to make decisions...

In summary, Schwartz's research leads him to make the following suggestions about making good decisions in a world where there are infinite choices:

- **Choose when to choose** – and when not to. Sometimes limiting your choice can be beneficial. Only let two or three options get on to your shortlist.
- **Actively define your criteria** – before getting bombarded with information from salespeople, adverts or magazines. Then seek the information you need to fulfil your criteria. I follow my parents' example when buying new appliances. I go to the library to consult whatever recent magazines they

hold that review whatever I am after (for example, a washing machine) and then shortlist two or three models according to the criteria that match my needs. Having found a review that I trust, I don't traipse round many showrooms and I don't spend hours trawling the internet. It works for me anyway. In the end, a washing machine is a washing machine to my mind. It's also how we made our last car purchase.

- **Consciously go for the "good enough" option**, in a world where there are plenty of equivalent goods or services. The chances are that most of them will be satisfactory so try not to agonise over the alternatives too much. School choice understandably sends most parents into maximiser mode, to try to find an elusive "best" for our children. The reality is that most children, given a supportive home life, will be all right in the end. I confess I've sort of got my fingers crossed as I even write that (dare I admit to wanting "good enough" for my children, rather than "the best"?!)
- **Anticipate adaptation.** You will get used to things once the novelty wears off. This can be seen as an opportunity to deepen your experience rather than trade in for something newer to keep the excitement up.
- **Try not to keep comparing with others.** This is difficult. But the more comparison you do with other people the more likely you are to be dissatisfied with your own lot, especially if you compare yourself "upwards". Maximisers are most likely to repeatedly do this in order to identify what "the best" is that they believe they should be aiming for.

Decisions in the neutral zone

Whilst in the neutral zone, be wary of making irreversible decisions. Leaping into action can seem very attractive. It gives off all sorts of signals to ourselves and others that we are in control of the situation and making tangible progress.

However, as things progress, people may find themselves wishing they hadn't acted so hastily. A relatively trivial example is when, within minutes of moving into a new house, people are ripping out the kitchen and remodelling the garden. It's so tempting and exciting.

Better decisions might actually be made however by spending some time with what's already there, and by floundering around in a "neutral zone" whilst you try different ideas for size (it may even take the form of literally camping depending on the state of the house). I've certainly heard more people say, later on, that they wish they hadn't rushed into whatever alteration they've done than I have heard those regretting spending a few months deciding what to do. Sleep on it.

In the neutral zone it is best to take your time; to make temporary decisions that don't slam other doors shut. Even though that can result in feeling less secure than you might like. Security is a slippery concept.

It may mean temporary jobs; or going out with someone rather than moving in with them; or renting a house in a new area for a while before buying a house.

It is fine, and indeed important, to do *something* though. This is a period of experimentation and a chance to try thing out. Being paralysed and doing nothing doesn't help you do that. It can take some courage, and some energy. Hence it is worth paying attention to the *Five Ways*, to support yourself through this time of transition.

Dale

Sarah is a chartered occupational psychologist and accredited coach, based in Nottingham, United Kingdom. She has designed a coaching programme called Creating Focus®, and more details can be seen on www.creatingfocus.org. She had a previous career with PricewaterhouseCoopers as a chartered accountant.

...usiness and psychology has turned out to be a ...tion although her eighteen year old self would ...aged (or welcomed) such a round-the-houses and ...reer path. Hindsight is a wonderful thing.

...th her husband, two daughters and step-son. ...y and challenge as you might expect in a family ...oy teenagers.

...ts include reading and writing; walking when ...nd her husband have a long term plan to walk ...t Coast Path in its 630 mile entirety – spread ...rs and pubs); daydreaming; sitting in coffee ...ting.

And on to the new beginning

New beginnings don't come with big flashing signs that tell you, unequivocally, that this is a new beginning. Very often instead they are accompanied by a growing sense that *this* is the right plan for you. There may even be an identifiable moment when you try an idea on and it seems to fit. And still feels like it does the next morning, and the morning after that.

As was clear at the beginning, we can never guarantee that this or that direction is going to be the cast iron one that can't go wrong. Stuff happens. There's a balance to be struck between waiting and trying alternatives until something feels right, and maximising (waiting for the perfect solution).

There is no perfect in most of our lives, it seems to me. There's great, there's exciting, there's pleasant, there's rewarding. Perfect seems illusory. You may argue with me but I think the concept of "Mr or Ms Right" is not particularly helpful. It implies that out of the billions of people in the world there is one – and only one – that you can be happy with. It's no wonder people get a bit worked up about trying to find him or her. Bit of a red herring if you ask me.

What to do if an idea fits and you suspect it is a lasting one that might herald a new beginning? Here are William Bridges' suggestions:

- **Stop getting ready and act.** Resist the temptation to maximise. Go with it. It doesn't have to be a decision for the whole of the rest of your life.
- **Identify yourself with the end result of the decision.** If it's a career change for example, imagine yourself in the shoes of that new profession or career.

- **Take things step by step** – some of which will seem insignificant at the time. There may be really hard work at this point; if you've decided to go to university in middle age for example and the idea fits, and keeps fitting, it may be the right new beginning for you. But there is still real work, and possible setbacks, in applying, being accepted, settling in and succeeding at university.
- Remember, none of this is static. We move through a whole variety of transitions, big and small, throughout our lives. Some we wrestle with, some we hardly notice. Some smack us in the face when we didn't want them, others we seek out.

As John F Kennedy put it, *"There is nothing more certain and unchanging than uncertainty and change."*

I find those words strangely comforting.

CHAPTER THREE – IN BRIEF

- Transition and change are part and parcel of life, and our sense of security can be something of an illusion.
- It is important to focus on taking care of yourself, using a model such as the *Five Ways to Well-being*, when you are in a turbulent situation. I think of it as camping.
- A model of transition such as that provided by William Bridges can give a reassuring way of negotiating change and uncertainty.

LEARN MORE

- www.neweconomicsfoundation.org – for more on the *Five Ways*, and www.foresight.gov.uk for the original report, Mental Capital and Well-being.
- *Transitions: making sense of life's changes* by William Bridges. Also see his website, www.wmbridges.com
- *The Paradox of Choice by Barry Schwartz* – entertaining and thought-provoking

A complete list of references can be found at the end of the book.

CHAPTER 4
A MENTAL BREAK (NOT BREAKDOWN)

A letter to my husband's iPhone

I know you are a sleek object of desire. I can see why. You have just come with us on a rare week's holiday for two in Greece. I was able to keep in touch with my daughters, on a family visit with their dad in the States.

I admit I am jealous of you. The way you capture his attention. The enthusiasm you generate with each new app. Sitting in an idyllic harbour side bar, sipping cocktails, I watched the moon rise as you kept us advised about the current cinema releases in our home town; about our ex-MP's new job in London; about a new bride on honeymoon on this very island falling off her balcony. I got drawn in. I flipped through an old university friend's holiday snaps (well, why not?) whilst whiling the time away on my own holiday.

I eavesdropped on other people's conversations, failing to manage to start one of my own. I can't compete. My knowledge of any subject isn't as thorough as yours; I ramble through half-formed opinions, you cut to the chase; my range of topics is repetitive and tiny by comparison. At times, churlishly, it occurred to me that an app for conversation prompts for married couples might be useful.

I can't keep nagging for you to be turned off; you're too useful and friendly. You are a hard act to follow. I can hear my own whine when each new location we reach is checked for Wi-Fi hotspots. I try to curb it: it's maybe no different from reading a book, and perhaps I'm a Luddite.

I love BBC Woman's Hour – but I don't want to listen to it whilst queuing for check-in in a hot and crowded Greek airport. I feel mean turning down the offer. Idle curiosity can be satisfied in an instant. "Exactly where is Cape Cod?" we wondered, thinking about my daughters. A few seconds later, there you were, zooming in to show us precise co-ordinates. "Amazing", we agreed, "what technology can do these days."

Over the past months, and on holiday, I have been practising mindful meditation. You seem to induce the opposite. Mindfulness is about being in the present, with what you perceive around you. You invite a wide-ranging awareness of random and infinite (often seductively interesting) events and facts from around the globe, or endless absorbing games. My mind is shouting STOP. I feel panicked, trapped in an insistent encyclopaedia. Mind full.

You won't remember the days when, in my childhood, it was part of the holiday ritual to look for a phone box, clutching a warm 10p coin to let grandparents know where we were. National radio quaintly made announcements for "Mrs So-and-so to call home immediately" in response to some family emergency. Now, you help us rest assured that all is well with our far flung loved ones as you would tell us instantly if they weren't. But in some ways that increases the anxiety. Perhaps something has happened in the five minutes since we turned you off. We might miss out on breaking news. Let's turn you back on again. In case.

And then we end up with so much news that we don't really need to hear. That clutters my dreams and interferes with our conversations. That stops us watching the moon rise.

I know I will own a version of you or your successors one day. I am (honestly) impressed by you. But, forgive me. I had to resist the urge to throw you into the harbour that week.

The rise of the "never off duty" work – and play - culture

Athletes understand the importance of not physically training to their utmost every day. Those at the top of their game will be very careful about when and how to rest, to step away from their sport even when they don't want to. Those who ignore this work harder than the others but won't sustain an elite position. They will incur more injuries and be more likely to burn out altogether. They end up stressed and out of control. They won't win prizes for pushing themselves harder than others (although they probably feel that they deserve to).

But most work cultures don't treat staff as elite athletes. Often far from it, instead we (consciously or not) expect to squeeze more and more from ourselves and others.

The technology and global nature of many aspects of life don't cause this in themselves (they are, despite appearances, inanimate objects that we choose to turn on). They are, however, very persuasive in encouraging dodgy assumptions about how effective we can be and for how long. They can give us an illusion of achieving more by heroic multitasking.

And they can lead to us forget that – collectively – we dictate the work culture in the end. Not vice versa.

Does this culture lead to "hurry sickness"?

Hurry sickness has been used to describe "Type A" personality – which is also conclusively linked to the likelihood of poor coronary health, as well as a poor quality of life. Does this description sound familiar of anyone you know?

"People who fit into this category are driven by a sense of time pressure to speed up the doing of all their daily activities and to do and think more than one thing at a time. They tend to be very poor listeners. They are constantly interrupting and finishing other people's sentences for them. They tend to be very impatient. They have great difficulty sitting and doing nothing or standing in lines, and they tend to speak rapidly and to dominate in social and professional situations." —Jon Kabat-Zinn

How is it for you?

These are some of the comments I've heard through the course of listening to my coaching clients. Do any of them ring bells for you?

- *There is no one else to do my work if I'm not around.*
- *I have to check emails on holiday because otherwise I would come back to so much work it wouldn't be worth going away.*
- *I can't stand my inbox to get overflowing so I work on it several times a day – every day – to keep on top of it.*
- *It's important that my team can get hold of me at any time – it's my job as a manager and I don't want to let them down.*
- *I'd rather deal with a crisis as it occurs than have it turn into something bigger on my return to work (after the weekend, an evening, a holiday).*

- *I'm expected to be available. My boss works long hours and we deal with overseas offices and customers which means we need to cover the time differences.*
- *I feel anxious if I haven't checked my phone and email frequently – there might be something I should have attended to and haven't.*
- *I can get ahead if I check emails and messages first thing in the morning or at weekends or in the evening.*
- *I love keeping in touch with everyone on Facebook, twitter and the like.*
- *I hate wasting time so the technology lets me be fully engaged in reading, listening, watching, talking wherever I am and whatever else might be going on.*
- *The range of interesting things I can stay up to date with via twitter, podcasts, websites, live streaming, iTunes…. makes me feel like a kid in a sweetie shop*
- *My new iPhone/Blackberry/new-generation-whatever is fantastic. Let me show you what it can do.*
- *I hate to look like I have nothing to do or no mates – so I'll always whip the phone out if I'm waiting for someone or there are a few minutes of down time.*
- *Everyone else works like this.*

Are we expecting ourselves and everyone around us to adopt a Type A personality? Is that the price we pay for the achievements in the twenty-first century workplace?

This isn't a rant against technology. It's truly extraordinary what is being developed and how it can, does and will enhance and impact on our lives, environment and future. But our brains and bodies aren't computers. They don't switch on or off like computers. They need a variety of activities and mental states to work – overall – at high capacity and optimum speed and quality.

What does taking a break mean?

It can mean anything from taking a ten minute break at work, to using your holiday allowance effectively, to taking a sabbatical from a long term demanding job. It might include what you do with weekends and evenings. It might mean how you balance family and other commitments. A forty hour working week still means there are 128 hours NOT at work.

It also might apply to taking a break from other things. Maybe including television, computers, social media, phones and all the things that are available for leisure and work. Maybe it includes taking a break from all-consuming projects like renovating an old house, or other responsibilities such as caring for children or elderly relatives. Or maybe even a break from your bid to be in the Olympic team.

This is not meant to imply that any of these, or other, absorbing activities is wrong or bad for you. But if you don't balance them with breaks of various sorts, you are very likely to become less effective in a whole variety of ways.

Let's count the ways you can lose effectiveness

- **Creativity** – can't see the bigger picture, or come up with innovative solutions to problems
- **Stamina** – can't be in it (whatever *it* is) for the long haul
- **Being engaged with your work** – stops feeling feel meaningful and purposeful
- **Decision making and judgement** – can become flawed with no breaks
- **Productivity** – don't achieve as much as you used to or want to
- **Relationships** – possibly self evident – but no breaks means little time for relationships. Working or personal.

- **Mental health**: stress, anxiety and depression. Burn out.
- **Physical health**: cardio-vascular health, and health related behaviours such as drinking, smoking, poor diet, lack of exercise that lead to poor health outcomes.

It seems to me that often as not, we won't even realise our mental health and cognitive capacities are being compromised by the way in which we are working or behaving. We are still functional, still achieving lots of things, still alert and interested. Or are we? Could it be different, better, more enjoyable or less painful?

....

What the experts say

"To stay alert and interested until the end of the working week, highly engaged persons need to detach from work when they are at home"

"Continuous preoccupation with work as a 24/7 approach to one's job is a double-edged sword that in the end might threaten employee health and well-being"
—Sabine Sonnentag, University of Konstanz

"Feeling recovered during leisure time, and positive work reflection, were related to an increase in performance over time"

"In weeks when individuals are highly recovered, they have more resources available that can be allocated to work tasks and thus benefit weekly performance"
—Carmen Binnewies, University of Mainz

"Enjoyable leisure activities are associated with psychosocial and physical measures relevant for health and well-being"

"The frequency of annual vacations by middle-aged men at high risk for coronary heart disease (CHD) [the type A's amongst others] is associated with reduced risk of all-cause mortality and, more specifically, mortality attributed to CHD"
—Sarah Pressman et al, University of Kansas

"Mindfulness meditation allows us to respond creatively to the present moment, freeing us from the knee-jerk reactions that start the cycle of rumination"
—Mark Williams, University of Oxford

....

Everyday breaks

1. Mindfulness

This is not a book or even a chapter about mindfulness, which is too big a subject to explore in depth here. There are many excellent books that can tell you a lot more than I can. However, it is a topic with rising popular interest and an increasing amount of robust scientific evidence of its benefits.

Mindfulness meditation is not the same as relaxation and is not a form of talking therapy. It has been shown to have a real impact in alleviating depression and anxiety. Evidence is also building that the benefits include resilience, creativity and better physical health.

What it can be described as is an awareness of our existence that is brought about by paying attention to experience in a particular way: on purpose, in the present moment and non-judgementally. It very often sounds easier than it is I might add.

It takes some practice – the eight week mindfulness based cognitive therapy for depression has been carefully formulated and tested by leading authorities in the field (see

Jon Kabat-Zinn, Mark Williams, or Rebecca Crane's books for a good start).

For now, the way in which mindfulness in general and mindful meditation in particular, can help provide a mental break is important. It's not about trying to empty your mind, or to switch off your very busy mental processes. And it's not a simplistic exhortation to live in the present. But what it does do – with practice – is lead to a state of mind which is highly effective at supporting all the activity that happens in the rest of our waking life. Those short breaks can be anything from three minutes to hours.

I personally find that ten minutes a day (most days) helps me to be more focused, calmer and, importantly, to pace myself more effectively. I think it does this by helping to counteract the mindless urgency that can so easily become a way of life, as well as leading to less time and energy spent worrying about past or future that is so often futile but so compelling.

I am still learning a great deal in this area, but I have read and experienced enough to keep me very interested in learning more.

2. Breaks in the daily grind

Your daily routine is important. Not that it has to be the same every day of course. But when everything blurs into one, it can lead to feeling as if you are at work all of your waking time. The fall-out for your own down-time as well as for time for relationships can be dramatic.

What's especially difficult for current working generations is that by and large we have to build our own boundaries. Previous generations could rely on external forces doing this for them: for example, the lack of decent electric light, or the prohibitive cost of overseas phone calls, or the Church's ruling.

Even in my life time there have been big changes. When I was a child, the television shut down at bed time. Shops were closed half day on Wednesdays and all day Sunday (my grandfather had a butcher's shop; we were well aware of the reality of fresh food retailing). No one could ring you whilst you were travelling, and no one could leave a voice message if you were out. Power cuts were fairly common. The internet wasn't even a twinkle in Tim Berners-Lee's eye (although it may have been starting to glow). And Mark Zuckerberg, founder of Facebook, wasn't even a twinkle in his parents' eyes. Organisations, often based around manufacturing, created tea breaks, lunch breaks and even shut down fortnights that were the same for the whole workforce.

True, we were bored some of the time (well, much of the time actually, as a teenager living in a village in the late seventies). It smacked of nanny-state at times.

But possibly it did mean – as a generalisation – that there was more opportunity for idle curiosity that wasn't instantly satisfied with a Google answer, and to give things full attention. I think it allowed space for creativity, relationship building, day-dreaming and concentration that, possibly, is missing for many of us today. There will of course always be great examples of all these things going on in any age; but are they as widespread for the average person as they once were?

Statistics on loneliness and mental health would suggest maybe not. I am not proposing that we should all look back to some mythical golden age. I don't think there ever has been such a thing (modern dentistry alone is enough to make me pleased I live now and not in the past). We tend to be very selective in looking back, but for good or ill things have changed radically over the years.

What I have observed is that many highly qualified, professional and desperately busy people can spend a great deal of time fire-fighting to correct things that have gone wrong as a result of not having enough thinking or decision-making time in the first place. Or they are often duplicating effort because there hasn't been time to find out what other people are doing.

All of this can lead to stressful deadlines and conflict, longer hours than strictly necessary and exhaustion.

Not to mention expending huge effort on things that might not actually be contributing to the highest priorities, for themselves or the organisation (a small but highly uncomfortable reflection).

Sometimes walking away, turning phones and computers off, going for a walk or playing with the kids or dog, can be precisely what's needed to solve a nitty-gritty problem.

....

Get some inspiration from others' inspirational breaks from work...

Maurice Wilkins, biophysicist at Kings College, London in the 1950's. Working on the then mystery of DNA, he had taken a photo that showed some kind of structure but couldn't work out what. Taking a break by going for a walk through London, he caught sight of the OXO tower. This led to the breakthrough needed – the X shape on the tower and in the photo led to the discovery of the double helix structure.

Fred Hoyle, astronomer and mathematician. The eureka moment for him came about by taking an evening off to go and see what was, by all accounts, a fairly terrible horror movie, *Dead of Night*. A 1940's horror version of *Groundhog Day*, revolving around recurring nightmares, it gave him the inspiration for his theory of how the universe began (I think the gist of which is that it didn't....no beginning or end....but I stand to be corrected).

(taken from the Channel 4 series *Genius of Britain*, produced by IWC Media)

....

3. Sleep

This is such a key part of a beneficial state of mind that there is a whole chapter devoted to it – see chapter 7.

Weekends

Traditionally, in recent decades, most people in the UK get two days off a week. But there are so many exceptions to this that it is hard to say what actually happens for most of us nowadays. For many people, once you build in a 24/7 culture, unpaid overtime, "just" checking emails, shift work, domestic and caring roles and everything else, it doesn't take the form of a Saturday/Sunday weekend.

I'm in no position to tell anyone how to spend their time, and as a coach and a writer I don't believe it is remotely helpful if I do (quite the opposite in fact). Any number of working and non-working patterns can work for people. However, if your patterns are leaving you feeling tired and emotional, it might be worth reviewing what's going on.

Here are a few of the sort of questions that I might ask in coaching sessions to help people reflect and inform their decisions. Make of them what you will.

- *What happens in your time away from work?*
- *What's your favourite way of spending a free day, and when did you last do that?*
- *How do you prioritise conflicting demands in a family or*

other group at the weekend?

- *Where do you keep your computer/phone/television etc?*
- *For what proportion of the weekend are these turned on and in use?*
- *Do you generally feel refreshed by your weekend?*
- *What makes it a good weekend?*
- *How do you negotiate who does what in terms of necessary chores and errands?*
- *How do you define what is actually necessary in terms of domestic and work related jobs that get done at home?*
- *Has working at home become a habit that is hard to break? – (but you find you can break it if there's something exceptional like a wedding to go to that takes up the whole weekend.)*

Holidays

Given how much money and energy we put into organising holidays, it might seem obvious that taking holidays is good for us. But it is also a common experience to feel as if you've never been away within about five minutes of getting back to work, and to wonder if it's all worth it. Especially if the holiday didn't live up to expectations and the effort required to clear the decks at work before and afterwards was immense.

There is, however, evidence that using your holiday allowance to actually take a break does have real benefits, whatever it might feel like at 10 o'clock on the first day back at work. This might seem like a revelation to those who don't see how they can take holidays, or don't want to, or have huge holiday balances rolled over year on year.

The measured benefits of taking holidays even extend to your life expectancy. Taking more holidays is linked to longer life expectancy. As with so much psychological and health research this is a correlation rather than a causal link but it does imply that a lifestyle including regular holidays is good for us.

So what does a holiday do?

The benefits of a holiday include:
- The provision of a space where the usual work stressors are not present – an avoidance of stress for a week or two.
- More opportunity for sleep.
- More opportunity for connecting with friends and family.
- A higher likelihood of fresh air and exercise.
- Probably better food and eating patterns.
- More opportunity for learning new things, seeing new places, for noticing things and being in the present.
- More time for conversation. And play.
- If it's your thing – maybe more chance to read for pleasure.

You might notice how similar this list is to the *Five Ways to Well-being*, mentioned in Chapter Three. It's no coincidence.

There is growing evidence of the benefits of holidays (see *what the experts say* above). There is not much research (yet) on what type of activity on holiday is best. However, the overall message seems to be:

When you are at work, work. When you're not at work, don't work.

In order to disengage from work when you are not at work, you probably need to do something that is fairly engaging in itself. This is why things like physical activity, music, conversation, hobbies, travel, games, sports and the arts are so enduringly popular. They engage our minds and bodies so that it is difficult to be worrying or thinking about something else at the same time. Holidays often embody lots of these things.

Don't be fooled by the apparent instant fading of your holiday when you get back to work. It IS still worth going.

So what's stopping you?

It's all very well. You may be totally convinced that short and longer breaks are good for you. If you're in a safety critical role that is regulated to provide for breaks you may be fine with it. But for lots of people it just doesn't happen.

Why not?

From the things I hear from people, I think it comes down to some underlying assumptions about ourselves and maybe some basic fears too.

- *If I take a break people will think less of me (I'm slacking, can't take the pace, am not committed and so on)*
- *If I take regular breaks, I won't get everything done I have promised to do. What drives you to promise more than you can deliver? Maybe if you don't, people will think you're not serious about your work, or they won't use your services again, or you'll get passed over for promotion. Or maybe you over-estimate how much you can realistically do.*
- *If I take breaks, I will lose track of what I'm doing.*
- *It's not worth taking longer breaks because of the work that piles up when I'm away.*
- *If I take breaks, I will let the team down. (They expect me to be superhuman/be available all the time/finish their work for them) Where have they got these expectations from? Where have you got them from?*

- *I run my own business, or am in a key role at work – I just can't be away from it. I cannot shut it down for a week or two. All sorts of unimaginable disasters could happen as a result (or actually, all sorts of only too imaginable disasters – I have imagined them all. In detail.).*
- *If I take breaks, I will leave myself with too much time to think and reflect on what I'm doing/how and why I do my job/how I live my life (and that is uncomfortable so it's better to fill the time with lots of work activity)*
- *If I take breaks I won't be as productive. This is a real mind-bending perception which can seem completely true. Athletes have to overcome this perception by getting lots of feedback on their performance and how it is affected by different factors including over-training. Mostly, in organisations or in professional jobs, we do not get that level of feedback so we don't realise we are becoming less productive or our performance is suffering – until we make a big mistake or fail to meet some deadline or delivery target. And the chances are everyone we work with is working in the same way so it's a bit of a blind leading the blind situation.*

How can you overcome some of these and take a break?

A shift of outlook first is the most helpful thing. Rather than imposing a load of rules about breaks and relying on will-power, remind yourself first that these breaks are important for you to be performing at your best, at work or elsewhere.

You probably wouldn't feel entirely relaxed if you knew that people in whom you place your trust for your personal safety haven't had an appropriate number and length of breaks: such as airline pilots and air traffic controllers; your doctor; the emergency services.

Taking a break is not an optional luxury for them, it is essential for long term performance – if you need or want to perform well, at work, home or just as a human, why should it be an optional luxury for you?

Take an experimental approach by trying different ideas and see what happens. Try them for two or three months at a time so you give it a good trial. Ask for feedback from your team or family or customers (or all of them).

Bit by bit, test out your assumptions about what disasters might befall you and your organisation if you take breaks. Note down how you feel before, during and after the experiment. Tweak your initiative as a result of feedback, from yourself and others. If it doesn't work, try something else.

Some ideas for taking a break experiments

- A change of scene – even for a few minutes. If you have been sitting at your computer screen for unbroken hours, get up and move around. There are software solutions to programme breaks in and remind you to stand up and change scene however briefly.
- Investigate some of the many approaches to mindfulness that are available (have a look in the references section at the end for some starters).
- Agree with other people to have a shared fifteen minute break. No agenda. Maybe start with doing this once a week if it can't happen every day. Stick to the time, don't let it drift. Make a point of noticing the effect this has over time.
- Get public transport more often. Being on a bus or train can give you some time off. Beware of automatically filling

that with work or news feeds or texts or whatever. Letting your mind drift for a while on its own can work wonders. It's worth noting that research shows that reading is a different thing from computer games or television as far as your brain is concerned so reading can be a good mental break from other things too.

- Decide when to turn things off. And do it.
- Don't have television or computers or trail your phone with you everywhere in the house.
- Book in time to have a chat or time with people if that's what it takes. Go to the cinema, for a bike ride, for a meal – whatever floats your boat (go in a boat if you like).
- Take the dog for a walk. Or pretend you've got a dog and just go for a walk; even if it's dark and raining. You would have to if you did have a dog, and we all accept that dogs are mammals and need this for their health. We are mammals too. Going with someone else can help to hit the relationship nurturing aspect too. Ten minutes, twenty minutes. Notice the change of seasons, and enjoy getting back in the warm and dry afterwards, if you've been dealing with a tempest outside.
- Be wary of multi-tasking. It often doesn't work. It's a bit of a modern mantra, which can make you feel busy and important; but also fragmented. And it can lead to being quite possibly slower and less good at everything.
- Ask for help if you need someone to cover your job or responsibilities for a period of time. Accept any help that is offered. There is little to be gained from being a martyr. You can always return the favour in some way at some future point.
- Book your holidays and treat them as sacrosanct. This working life thing is a marathon not a sprint, and you have

to pace yourself if you are going to stay the course (and lord knows, with the current pension economy it might be quite a long course).

- Have at least one day a week without any work related activities. No email. No phone calls. No "just" having a look over this or that. Hide your laptop and briefcase. In the words of the seventies children's show "go and do something less boring instead".

And here's an idea for an "in work" break

Professor Barbara Dexter, of Derby University, has pioneered the three day writing retreat for academics. As in most universities, the research output in terms of writing, publishing and conference presentations is a key measurable performance indicator. Academics are under pressure for their own careers and for the reputation of their institution to be actively engaged in research, but not surprisingly, finding time to concentrate on writing up that research can be a challenge.

The retreat takes place annually for up to 32 staff on a voluntary basis. They head off to a local(ish) hotel/training centre (Scalford Hall in Melton Mowbray if you're really interested, which is far enough from Derby to be hard to pop into the office, but not so far you're travelling for a day at each end).

They meet for checking in with each other and goal setting at the beginning of each day. There are set break times which are optional but which mean that those who want to (which is most people) have a break, a coffee, and lunch together. The Danish pastries are a key part of the process too, I am told.

Everyone then heads back to their notebooks and laptops, for four distinct writing sessions a day, followed by dinner together in the evening.

The output which participants say is directly attributed to the 2009 retreat is 8 journal publications; 11 conference papers; a national radio appearance; a book and 17 other related research outputs (such as chapters in books).

What's attributed to the retreat?

In addition to the publications above, who knows how many staff speak highly of the University outside of its walls as a result of this (and what impact that has)? Who knows how many lecturers didn't leave or go off sick because they had this experience? Who knows how many cleared their minds long enough to have big ideas, of benefit to themselves and the university (and to the rest of us)?

We can't measure everything because we don't tend to live in controlled experiments (much as, I admit, psychologists might like that). Measuring the effect we didn't get from the road we didn't take is difficult.

The less measurable effects on mental health; working relationships (and I would guess home relationships too); confidence; motivation and cross institutional networks are arguably the most important longer term outcomes. We'll probably never know for sure.

But I leave you with some of the things that staff involved in this retreat said. Maybe their words resonate with you.

I met staff from the University I had never come across before and we shared experience, practice and knowledge.

It was a worthwhile experience that benefits the organisation through what I put back and me for what I have got out of it.

Having direct access to support from more experienced colleagues.

The retreat gave me the space to gather my thoughts, pull various elements together, put many words to paper and come up with something about 60% complete. Some of the understanding I gathered then inspired a workshop I then delivered at a conference.

The retreat was extremely useful in sketching out the early stages of the chapter and structuring its argument.

A feeling of others undertaking work at the same time helped.

The article I knocked up over the writing retreat is going to be a point of discussion on Radio 4.

It was good to have time to write which was undisturbed so that one could write with flow.

It was just what I needed and has since motivated me forward particularly since my co-editor's sudden and unexpected death a month before the retreat which knocked me for six.

I found the retreat inspirational in finishing off the paper I have been working on for some time. The company was excellent, interesting to meet such a diverse range of academics and to identify a similar like-mindedness amongst us.

I like the agenda: non-intrusive, focuses the mind and makes you feel a part of something.

One part of the year where I have no excuses and no distractions.

Something quite magical in being in a lovely building, in the middle of a beautiful landscape and being able to read and write – a wonderful opportunity and a real privilege

It was one of the highlights of my working year.

I would suggest that we can all take a leaf out of this particular book. The nature of our work might be different, but less is more sometimes. Cutting back on the distractions, and putting support in place to do that, can mean that you spend fewer hours working on something but they are much higher quality hours. Calm and considered input, with appropriate breaks, at a planning or thinking stage can have a major beneficial payback later.

Work when you are working. And don't when you are not.

CHAPTER FOUR – IN BRIEF

- Taking breaks is not an optional luxury if you want to be performing well in the longer term. Breaks are a necessity.
- Having time and ways of actively disengaging from work is important to keep the quality of your work high.
- There are a range of cultural and work related pressures that mean people don't take breaks. It can be useful to take an experimental approach to try to challenge those.

LEARN MORE

- www.bemindful.co.uk – the mindfulness site from the Mental Health Foundation
- www.getsomeheadspace.com – Andy Puddicombe is the face and voice of this organisation, which has been featured in many publications and programmes and brings mindfulness to many workplaces.
- *Mindfulness-based cognitive therapy* by Rebecca Crane. I did some training with Rebecca (who is at Bangor University) which was very useful and interesting.
- *The Mindful Way through Depression* by Mark Williams, John Teasdale, Zindel Segal and Jon Kabat-Zinn – includes guided meditation on a CD and Mark is one of the UK's leading researchers and practitioners in the mindfulness field.
- *Full Catastrophe Living* by Jon Kabat-Zinn – a worldwide best-seller on the subject.

A complete list of references can be found at the end of the book.

CHAPTER 5

FRIENDS AND ACQUAINTANCES

Subject:	*How's things?*
Sent:	*Tuesday 25/05/2010 21.09*
To:	*katherine.smith@xxxxxx.com*

Hi there,

How are you keeping? It seems ages since we spoke – no excuses here apart from the usual one of being so busy. Work is a bit of a nightmare of late – we're all working long hours but to be honest I'm not sure what on....(better not admit that to the boss though!). The kids are ok but we're going through it a bit with Natalie, she seems to have hit teenage-hood early, I wasn't ready for this at nine! Rob's ok though he is worried about work too, there's been one round of redundancies so far and he seems sure there'll be another one before the end of the year too. We're keeping going though, nothing to complain about compared to some people. Though I have to say that doesn't seem to stop us moaning!

Although I haven't been in touch for such a long time, it's not that I haven't thought about you! How is your Mum? I really hope things have improved there. Must be very difficult for you all. And I'm sorry I missed your birthday. And is Dave pulling his weight with the kids? Shall we make superhuman efforts and try to meet up one evening soon? The drinks are definitely on me.

Lots love, Sue

....

Re: **How's things?**
Sent: *Thursday 27/05/2010 22.14*
To: *S.Lyon@yyyyyy.com*

How great to hear from you! I've been meaning to get in touch for ages too but somehow other things keep getting in the way.

Mum really isn't well at all now and is going through another round of chemo – we're all keeping our fingers crossed but Dad is finding it especially difficult. I try to get there every week but it's not easy. Dave's being really unhelpful with having the kids when I need him to as well – did I tell you his girlfriend has moved in with him? The children liked her at first (which is more than I did – but I have only met her once in a car park if I try to be fair...don't really feel like being fair though) but now she seems to be putting all sorts of rules in place about when they'll have the kids which means I can't always leave the kids to see Mum so it's pretty stressful at times. Anyway, not much of a topic for email so I'll tell you more when I see you.

Otherwise things seem to be going along ok though I feel so tired all the time I sometimes find it hard to even lift the wine bottle!! Maybe my age is catching up, we never used to have that problem! Work is carrying on as usual – another reorganisation under way so as usual no one seems to know what's going on – but I guess I count myself lucky to have a job at the moment.

Anyway, going to have to keep this short, I've got to dash to pick Tom up from football (he's in the school team now, I have to do that parental thing on the sidelines some Sunday mornings – never thought I'd see the day) – great idea to go out, when is a good time?

Love, Kx

....

Re: *How's things?*
Sent: *Friday 18/06/2010 18.24*
To: *katherine.smith@xxxxx.com*

OMG!! Sorry it's taken SOOOOO long to reply. The cat was ill and we had to have her put down in the end but that's not good enough reason. Sorry.

And I'm so sorry to hear about your Mum. These things are terrible.

I'll keep this short, we should talk in person, so much to tell you – are you free to go out next Thursday?

Suex

....

Re: *How's things?*
Sent: *Friday 18/06/2010 23.53*
To: *S.Lyon@yyyyy.com*

Don't think I can go out on Thursday. Mum has been admitted to the hospice. Will keep you posted. Kx

....

Subject: *One-nil*
Sent: *Monday 15/11/2010 9.03*
To: *Paul.simpson@aaaaa.co.uk*

Enjoyed the game on Saturday? I don't like to gloat but... Matt

....

Re: *One-nil*
Sent: *Monday 15/11/2010 9.24*
To: *M.R.Wright@bbbbb.ac.uk*

We'll be back. The drinks will be on you. I will laugh. P

....

Re: *One-nil*
Sent: *Friday 19/11/2010 17.11*
To: *Paul.simpson@aaaaa.co.uk.com*

Fancy a pint on the way home? Give me a chance to gloat in person! Matt

....

Re: *One-nil*
Sent: *Friday 19/11/2010 17.32*
To: *M.R.Wright@bbbbb.ac.uk*

A cracking idea (gloating aside, I will deal with that later).
But unfortunately can't – Amanda is going out tonight and I'm on baby sitting duty – will be baby sitting for whole of next year if I'm not home on time. Another time? Paul

....

Crowded lives

Crowded lives don't allow for much in the way of friendship. Or time to invest in relationships, whether with friends, family, neighbours or colleagues. The email exchanges above are fictional, but they are typical of the level of communication I've seen and heard about (and been involved in) between people whose intentions are good but the reality of day to day life gets in the way.

Despite all the means of communication that we have these days, it is still quite possible to lose touch altogether; one house move too many, a new mobile phone number, a change of job and/or email address and it can be difficult to keep track.

One of the most common reflections I hear in coaching work is that people would like more time to see their friends, but their own (and their friends') pressures of work and family usually mean there isn't time or energy left to meet up with people.

This chapter will look at whether this matters, other than leaving us feeling a bit wistful. It suggests some ideas for re-connecting with people, or making new connections, if you decide you want or need to.

Solitude versus loneliness

"Loneliness is not about being alone but a subjective experience of isolation."
—The Lonely Society, Mental Health Foundation 2010

We often spend a lot of our time surrounded by others, at work and possibly at home too (although single person households are on the rise; they represented 12% of households in Britain in 2008). The legacy we leave is usually something to do with our relationships: as a parent, or spouse, or child. If you have a look around a cemetery for a few minutes, you will find that there aren't many gravestones commemorating someone as a manager or administrator or director for example. One of the most appealing epitaphs I have heard was "He or she had a genius for friendship".

At the same time, it is common to hear people craving time away from it all (and from everyone else). The romantic idea of beating a retreat to the countryside, or pulling up the drawbridge to recover your equanimity alone is a widespread, and appealing, one.

There is of course nothing at all wrong with solitude. Many of us need that at times in our lives and it is a great thing to be happy with your own company. Certainly I enjoy the feeling of having the house to myself. But solitude and loneliness are very different things.

Houses are designed, as are so many other aspects of life in a modern Western society, with privacy and individual needs as over-riding concerns. You may never have to share.

Multiple en-suite bathrooms (at the expense of storage or living space); at least one mobile phone each (so you never need be overheard making a call); a TV in every room (saves the arguments over what to watch); our own cars (more comfortable than sharing a bus or train with strangers); shopping on line; detached houses (always sold at a premium); social media (so there is arguably less need or opportunity to interact face to face); a growing social taboo on just dropping in on people (when did you last drop in uninvited to someone outside of your family? Or someone drop in on you? And how did you feel if they did?).

As Philip Slater, in an old but still relevant book called *The Pursuit of Loneliness* (1970), said,

"We seek more and more privacy, and feel more and more alienated and lonely when we get it."

This all seems to be linked to busy-ness too. We respect other people's busy-ness, and don't want to impinge on them. We believe whole heartedly in our own. It is seen as an admission of some kind of social failure if you are NOT busy. Why would you have time on your hands if you were productive and useful and popular?

Being unemployed and/or lonely often induces a real sense of shame, and people will sometimes go to great lengths to cover these up (remember the unemployed manager Gerald in the film *The Full Monty*?). And yet being lonely is a very common state that can happen to any of us at some time in our lives. Loneliness is unequivocally linked to mental health problems.

Does loneliness matter?

Physical health

"The degree of social connection has significant effects on longevity, on an individual's response to stress, on the robustness of immune functions, and on the incidence and course of a variety of specific illnesses."
—Jacqueline Olds and Richard S Schwartz, *The Lonely American*

Lonely people are nearly twice as likely to die in any ten-year period than those who feel well connected to other people (this is especially the case for men).

This is after controlling for health related behaviours such as drinking and smoking. It is thought that social connection with other people is the second most important influence on our health – after the influence of our genes in general – so arguably even more important for our health than exercise or nutrition.

How does loneliness harm our health?

The Mental Health Foundation put together an excellent report in 2010 on loneliness. They summarised the health effects as follows:

- Lonely people find it harder to regulate their health behaviour. Loneliness erodes will-power over things like drinking, exercise, smoking, over-eating.
- Middle-aged people in particular report feeling more exposed to stress if they are also feeling lonely
- Lonely people are likely to get into a vicious cycle of withdrawing from others and be less likely to seek social support – hence feeling worse
- Loneliness affects the cardio-vascular and immune systems in a negative way
- Loneliness can affect sleep quality which then has other knock on effects on our health (see chapter 7).

Stress

Lack of social support and connection has been shown to be a critical part of our experience of stress. Mountains of research with different groups of people in different countries and times have demonstrated this. Our own experience backs these findings up.

Historically, groups in a position to decide such things have known that solitary confinement is one of the worst forms of punishment people have been able to devise. That's saying something given the imaginative ways people have come up with to hurt each other over the centuries.

I remember John McCarthy (taken hostage in Beirut in the eighties, along with Terry Waite and Brian Keenan) reflecting what a difference it made to the situation he was in once he was held captive with Brian rather than alone. The situation hadn't changed, it was still terrifying and just about no element of it was within their control; but the negative emotions were held in check more effectively with company.

Almost any challenging experience is more challenging if you have to face it on your own (that is, I admit, the kind of sentence that will immediately encourage you to think of all the exceptions).

You may have some preference over *who* you face the challenges with; but even when you haven't that luxury, people cope better with others. As I write this, the world is watching the horrific unfolding of events following the massive earthquake and tsunami in Japan (March 2011). Any of the stories emerging just emphasise the importance of supporting each other, whether strangers or not. We are a social species, and, with very few exceptions, stronger for it.

The big emotions in the experience of stress are fear and anxiety. Both have very fertile ground in lonely people, who have a lot of opportunity to ruminate without the reassurance, perspective or help that other people can bring. Being lonely is a fearful, anxious process in itself.

Living in a cocoon

Jacqueline Olds and Richard Schwartz are psychiatrists at Harvard Medical School, and authors of a book called *The Lonely American: drifting apart in the twenty-first century*.

One of the trends they have seen in patients and families they deal with is that of "cocooning". It rang a bell for me with the people I meet through the course of my work and elsewhere and is partly, I think, a result of the crowded lives that we all recognise.

Cocooning describes families and especially married couples who, caught in very time pressured lives, just don't maintain a wider social circle outside of their marriage or family. This may be intentional up to a point or just an effect of losing touch with people. It may also be a reflection of the cultural expectation many people have in modern western societies of being their partner's "best friend"; and even extending that to their children too (a mistake, I think, but that is probably another book).

It can be difficult to make new friends as an adult too. External factors such as frequent relocations or the structure of neighbourhoods can make it tricky. And internal factors such as not wanting to appear needy or weak are probably even more powerful influences.

The structures many of us live in enable this to happen very easily. Most of us, once laden with jobs and responsibility, don't venture out of the house for a social life in the way that maybe previous generations did. In addition, we don't have to go out for entertainment, there's so much available at home now.

Post-war paternalistic companies commonly provided sports and social clubs, bars, canteens and outings for their staff and their families. I knew someone who used to work at Raleigh (of bicycle fame) here in Nottingham. With over 8000 people working there in its heyday, there was a thriving social scene there with facilities provided by the company. Not always a trouble-free experience, I'm sure, but loneliness may not have been the biggest concern. Some of the parties sounded like a blast.

Part of the issue of cocooning within a marriage or nuclear family is that there is a lack of social witnesses to the relationship. It is this, Olds and Schwartz argue, that can lead to a gradual decline in how well we treat each other, and to feeling very lonely within a marriage or family. In extreme terms, it is known that abuse is more likely to occur in isolated families. On a more day to day level, most of us know that some of our least fine moments have happened behind the privacy of our own front doors.

An element of maintaining those tricky long term relationships and bringing up children successfully is done by effectively performing for other people, as well as by having some reference points gained from seeing other couples and families in action. It's also important to have a circle of friends and acquaintances that you can confide in outside of the marriage or family, and who can empathise and share their experiences.

After all, most of us are making it up as we go along when it comes to these core relationships and child rearing. We need all the help we can get.

Olds and Schwartz conclude:

"A marriage is most likely to flourish when it is woven into a larger tapestry that includes extended family, friends, neighbours and peers."

Whilst time with your partner and children is important, and deliberate cocooning can be relaxing and fun for short periods, you will (perhaps counter-intuitively) strengthen it best by not prioritising it to the exclusion of time with other people.

An important point to note is that you don't necessarily have to get on with those people like a house on fire. Let's face it; other people can be irritating at times. But the contact with them from time to time is still good for you. Even, it would appear, if those other people are annoying relatives or needy neighbours.

Being left out

Being left out is one of the strongest threats we can experience. Ranging from not having anyone to sit next to during school meal times, to being sent into exile, the overwhelming power of the threat of being left out just highlights how strong our urge to belong is.

It doesn't even come from *actually* being left out. The *perception* that you're being left out is just as powerful; even if you're not, from a more elusive objective stance. And it can seem like a childish feeling that, as adults, we should have grown out of. We've (mostly) all been there at some time or other, most commonly in our teen years. But it's a strong, instinctive and unpleasant feeling at any age.

It turns out that feeling socially excluded can have some serious consequences for our own well-being (and probably that of other people). This includes:

- Being more aggressive
- Creating self-defeating behaviour (procrastination, unhealthy eating and so on)
- Reducing cognitive functions – a decline in reasoning abilities
- More likely to give up on challenging tasks

(Studies by Twenge and Baumeister, reported in *The Lonely American*)

It appears that our personal and group survival has depended on a very ancient, biological urge to belong, which means that we are therefore hyper-vigilant against feeling left out. It is a very easily triggered form of distress.

A note on individual differences: people vary

As a psychologist, this is something I am reminded of and try to keep in mind all the time. One size of approach definitely does not fit all. In relation to social connection, personality differences (whether they came from nature or nurture) serve to mean we vary greatly from one person to the next as to how much social contact we want or need.

I find the Myers Briggs Type Indicator to be a useful and reliable framework to describe personality differences and often use this with the people I coach. One dimension of this is the introvert-extravert scale. This does not refer to how confident or loud people are, but relates to where they get their energy from; essentially in what ways they recharge their batteries. Extraverts are likely to seek out other people and are re-energised by that contact: the gossip, the noise, the buzz. Introverts, by contrast, need more time alone or with a few close friends or family to re-charge (solitude not loneliness).

One is not better than the other or more related to loneliness than the other. Either extreme can experience loneliness, and either can enjoy time alone or with others. What it will mean is that people at various points along this scale will have different ideal balances between comfortable time alone and enjoyable contact with others.

There is some emerging research from social neuroscientists that this preference may be set by our early life experiences, to set us a gauge for how much social contact we feel comfortable with. Who knows where it comes from? It doesn't much matter here. The important thing is that you may be different from others you know. That's fine. The trick lies in understanding what works for you.

How to benefit from contact with other people

- **Friendship needs nurturing.** There is some risk that it might not seem like time or effort well spent. I have heard it said that as a rule of thumb you should expect to issue three times as many invitations as you receive to keep a good network going. That starts to sound like hard work. Of course it's usually not that calculated. But if your friendships seem to be dropping by the wayside it might be worth reviewing. Taking up interests such as sports, music or community roles where you have an easier "way in" to new groups can be a very effective strategy too.

- **Expectations need to be realistic.** Soap operas and TV series such as *Friends* make it look like people deal with conflict quickly and fairly easily, and they frequently hit intense moments of emotional connection. I've yet to meet anyone whose friendships are quite like that. But if you have that as a model of friendship then all the real friendships might seem a bit – well – *boring* by comparison. It takes time and patience (and probably a fair few misunderstandings on the way) to form long term friendships.

- **Tolerance.** Not all of the people you spend time with will be your best mates. Other acquaintances (and maybe even family) can be people you have little in common with. But there does seem to be something about the wider mix and contact that is beneficial. It may not always be people you even like that much, or know that well. However, the contact can still be meaningful and help to form that sense of being part of something: your organisation, your community or your family. You never know, you might discover those people have some saving graces. Be careful about cutting people out too readily, knowingly or not.

- **Assertiveness.** As a counter-balance to tolerance, it is also important to be clear about where you do want your boundaries to be. None of this is about accepting that all of your time is taken over by other people. In fact, most of us in a franticly busy world have a fear of that happening and so tend to keep our distance in the first place, in case we are overwhelmed. We can often define that boundary for ourselves by being clear with others, and this doesn't have to be rude or unkind. It's not either no contact or way too much, but somewhere in the middle - which brings me on to the next point.

- **Striking a balance** between enjoyable solitude and a sense of belonging that brings us perspective and support in the longer term is what we're after I guess. The drive to step back from contact because many of us are so busy is powerful. But step back too far (bit by bit) and you can realise you feel left out and lonely. I think this is what can happen when some of the people I meet profess to hate all work related social events and to avoid other gatherings too. Some of them may be truly introverted and that's fine. However, I suspect some are taking more and more steps back to try to limit their busy-ness and find some peace and quiet. This runs a risk of realising, possibly much later, that they have lost some of the benefits of that run of the mill, not necessarily always congenial, contact.

Phone a friend

This is about half way through the book.

Why not take a break and phone a friend, or invite someone for a coffee, or have a chat with someone in your house, street or work? Most of us have someone whose name has been running round our minds as someone we haven't been in touch with for a while.

Maybe this could be the prompt to do something about it. Just a thought.

CHAPTER FIVE – IN BRIEF

- We need social contact with others for our psychological health.
- It's one of the first casualties of very busy lifestyles for many of us.
- Family life benefits from being part of a wider network, not an isolated unit. The same applies to couples.

LEARN MORE

- *The Lonely American* by Jacqueline Olds and Richard Schwartz. This is a very readable account of the growing social isolation that they have observed in American culture during their careers as psychiatrists, now both with academic as well as clinical roles at Harvard Medical School. My observations would suggest that it's not that different in the UK. Olds and Schwartz point out that in our culture today it can be more socially acceptable to be depressed than lonely. That strikes me as a real pause for thought. They have also written *Marriage in Motion* which is outside the scope of this book but interesting nonetheless.
- *The Lonely Society?* was a report and campaign by the Mental Health Foundation in 2010. The report can be downloaded from their website, www.mentalhealth.org.uk, along with suggestions for tackling it.

A complete list of references can be found at the end of the book.

CHAPTER 6

HOW TO HAVE A CONVERSATION

"A single conversation across the table with a wise person is worth a month's study of books"
—Chinese Proverb

"A single conversation is worth a thousand emails"
—My version

Ask almost any manager (or anyone else) in an organisation what they would most like to see improved and they nearly always say communication. It is practically a truism that communication can always be improved. We have more ways of communicating, faster and with further reach than ever before: email, social networking, mobile phones and texts, letters, postcards, landlines, skype, short range radio, television, radio, newspapers and magazines, books, podcasts, town criers, newsletters, e-zines, semaphore, Morse code, pigeons, messages in bottles.

And talking and listening face to face.

Still it is not enough. Or is it actually too much?

Either way, something feels as if it has to give for many busy people at work.

This chapter will look at the drawbacks and benefits of conversation; the skills and context required to maximise the chances of a good conversation; the difference between conversation and moaning; and some suggestions for building in conversation as a key part of your working life.

Let's start with the drawbacks

Why *wouldn't* you seek to have a conversation with someone about something? Why do we often keep quiet, or email instead, or let assumptions and misunderstandings cloud our thinking about an issue?

- It might take up too much time. A constant sense of being too busy accompanies many of us, all day every day. How much of it is a perception and how much of it is reality? How much control do you have over it? Is it a modern taboo to not be busy some of the time?
- It might mean you get caught up listening to boring or negative endless moaning (the "water cooler conversations"). Or worse, have to get involved in the detail of the latest gripe (the car parking arrangements, the Christmas party...)
- It might develop into an argument if you know you have different views or approaches from someone else.
- It might be embarrassing. There might be emotional issues or awkward silences. You might not know what to say, or might not want to hear what the other person has to say.

The power of these drawbacks

The drawbacks are powerful. Any of these, or some kind of horror combination of several of them, can stop you in your tracks before you even get started. If, for example, you're anticipating a lengthy confrontation with tears and criticism over the Christmas party plans, you're likely to stay well clear.

Add to this your own personality preferences and you might find it very difficult to start a conversation or to choose a conversation over the many other ways of communicating.

The introversion-extraversion scale as defined in the Myers Briggs Type Indicator (as I referred to in Chapter 5) can influence the way in which you might approach others. Added to that, people vary in how shy or not they may be. It may be an odd mix, but I am something of a shy extravert. That's not actually that unusual. I very much get a buzz from other people, and love few things as much as great conversation, but can sometimes feel reticent or self-conscious about making the first move.

Finding ways to communicate that play to your strengths is a good strategy. But it's also worth being aware of when your preferences may be actually acting against you and holding you back.

So what about the benefits?

The drawbacks can present quite a hurdle. But if you manage that, the benefits can be colossal. The key ones:

- **The connection with other people.** Whether this is colleagues, your boss, your family members, people you like or people you don't like, it provides the basis for a link with others on a one to one basis. The amount of information provided by a conversation goes way beyond the words themselves. The body language, the facial expressions, the reactions to what you have said, the tone and way in which sentences are communicated all give you a rich picture of what that person intends to convey.

The social anthropologist Professor Robin Dunbar suggests that the role of gossip is a bonding ritual for humans that creates groups much as grooming does for primates. This is essentially conversation that is *not* purely functional and task related, but is simply a nice chat. I'm sure that cafes and pubs must therefore be part of this bonding ritual too; which means that it's perfectly justified for our mental health to hang out in them, to my mind. It's good to have cleared that one up anyway.

- **Conversation saves time in the end.** Despite the real fears that it uses up time in an uncontrolled manner, good quality conversation remains one of the most efficient ways we have of communicating and thinking. It can be quicker to thrash out new ideas; to understand different perspectives; to build teams and working relationships; to pass on information; to understand information; to see the bigger picture.

  Conversation provides the opportunity for short cuts to occur in tasks; whilst talking about something it is common for the other person to be reminded of something that may help you. I come away from so many conversations with references or tips on how to approach anything from work related activities to bringing up teenagers.

  Even in our modern world, word of mouth is often the fastest and most effective way to spread news or information that can lead to the great insight or revelation that you are looking for in your work. You might well miss that if you're always too busy for a conversation.

- **Conversation provides the opportunity to think things through properly.** A good conversation, with a focused exchange of ideas, can let the rest of the world slip away from view for a while. It gives you a chance to develop your ideas, to have to explain them well, to realise when you haven't made yourself understood and to find new ways of expressing your thoughts. It is more memorable than a stream of emails, and more energetic and creative than more distant communication methods. It also gives scope for your ideas to be challenged, for you to develop your arguments for your case, or to seek reassurance that you are not alone in what you are thinking.

- **It builds trust and respect** – a solid foundation for future business and personal relationships. This can be despite differences of opinion. In fact good conversation can build the framework for handling those differences and for taking you or the business through sticky times when morale or trust are at a low ebb.

Maximising your chances of a good conversation

Like anything else, there are skills and circumstances that will help. Conversation needs practice (like most things).

How many decent conversations do you have in an average week?

Once you have battled through the emails, rushed from meeting to meeting, got home late and exhausted, there can seem little opportunity. It's not for want of a conversation, it's just that for many people life has got to a pitch that makes it difficult to hold an undivided conversation and pay full attention to it.

And I think there's the rub. I hear people having conversations on mobiles all the time of course; but they are also travelling, or doing the washing up, or feeding their children or whatever else they have to do. The statistics for how many phone conversations are allegedly held when at least one party is sitting on the toilet can give you some pause for thought before you ring a team member outside of office hours.

Conversation versus moaning

People, especially busy people, can sometimes shy away from conversation in case it turns into a liturgy of moaning. Or alternatively they get drawn to the Big Moan and join in at length. This happens. Many organisations have their favourite topics for moaning: Head Office doesn't understand us; the sales team make impossible promises; if only "they" would resolve the car parking, the office heating system, the overtime arrangements and so on. Somewhat ironically, often the favourite ongoing moan is all about how busy or tired everyone is. It can develop into a competition very easily. And can take up hours of time and huge amounts of energy.

There is no immediate answer to this other than to be well aware of when this is happening and what your reaction might be. I had one client who realised that he was the kind of person that people confided in (which was a good thing – up to a point). Unconsciously this had led to him being drawn into any number of "moans". In a big and complex organisation, there was precious little he could do about the perennial topics even though he was in a senior position. It dragged him down. But he felt as if it was part of his duty and wish as a decent manager to listen to all of this, and indeed to join in.

Once more aware of it though, he was able to see it a little more objectively. We can all choose how to react to these issues. Changing habits is difficult but not impossible. You can be polite to people without getting deeply caught up in their angst. List out what you can influence and what you can't. If you can't influence something, try to keep to the minimum of moans about whatever it is. Limit the time you are exposed to this. All that will do is erode any positive energy you might have.

Have some questions up your sleeve that can replace these moans with conversations that focus on issues that you and the person talking to you *can* do something about. However small or trivial they might seem.

Some suggestions

- **Cut down on the distractions.** Pretending to listen to someone whilst emails are pinging in within sight or your phone is flashing and vibrating on the table between you is not effective. I think it can be quite rude too. Find a quieter place or somewhere with comfortable background noise (another plug for coffee shops).

- **Manage how much you are overheard.** Even if the conversation is not particularly sensitive or confidential, it is inhibiting for people to feel that others are listening in. Beware of the speaker phone for that reason. I once worked in an office where a senior manager always put the phone on speaker phone so that he was hands free to take notes. It meant the unwitting (usually junior) person at the other end was being broadcast into the unknown. I had unwillingly listened in to some of these conversations if I happened to be in the room when the phone rang. Very uncomfortable. I've also unwillingly listened in on hands-free phone conversations as a passenger in a car. The person they are talking to doesn't know if there's anyone else in the car, and this seems fraught with potential difficulties to me. And as for some of the uninhibited work-related phone conversations that go on in trains ... well, I probably don't need to say more. Remember that you might be comfortable with everyone else hearing it all but others might not – whatever the topic.

- **How long have you got?** Manage expectations for everyone involved. Say at the outset that you have to be finished by x time. If a chance conversation looks like it is developing further and you both want it to, suggest you retire to somewhere more congenial or arrange to meet up again rather than standing in the corridor or street.

- **Listen.** So obvious. But how many of us *really* listen well, and how frequently? There are so many other things on our minds and so many interruptions. As a quick reminder, listening skills include the following:

  Eye contact and body language that indicate to both of you that you are paying attention. This varies slightly between cultures and there is no one set of "rules" – but others will know when you're not genuinely listening.

  Letting the person finish their train of thought (or at least their sentence). Countless arguments arise and get more heated because no one is letting anyone else finish – and this, as we all know, is incredibly frustrating. Even if someone appears to be very long-winded, they will only become more long-winded if you keep trying to hurry them up and finish off for them.

  Say small things that indicate you are listening: occasional affirmations, or summaries of what you've heard, or ask relevant questions that help you to clarify what you are hearing.

- **Conversations in the car** can be surprisingly fruitful. It is something to do with the captive audience I think. Travelling with colleagues to meetings can be a good opportunity for this.

- **Talking and walking** can also sometimes be good (British weather notwithstanding). It can be a way of getting into a subject in a relaxed way. A colleague and I introduced this in a complex group facilitation where we needed to encourage communication in a multi-disciplinary group of people, who were meeting with the aim of improving the look and use of green spaces in an inner city. What better way to begin what were sometimes difficult conversations than to walk around the nearest park?

- **Are you leaving some people out?** Maybe some colleagues, friends or family members are quieter or seem self-contained or just get on with things. This is not about forcing conversation on those who really don't want it, but it's easy to overlook the people who are not grabbing your attention.

- **Manage your own expectations** about what can be achieved. Sometimes a conversation can be life changing. But more often than not it is one piece in a complicated jigsaw. It may just be a chance to understand a little more around a particular topic. It may just be a chance for one of you to get something off your chest. It may appear to have done nothing other than take the lid off a can of worms. But keep the faith. Even if you can't see what good it might be doing, the chances are you are edging closer to beneficial outcomes than if you didn't have a conversation.

CHAPTER SIX – IN BRIEF

- Conversation can become lost in the multi-tasking, high technology world we live and work in.
- It can still be the most effective way of communicating.
- Benefits include: building trust and relationships; understanding an issue more fully; working your own ideas out; it can be enjoyable and meaningful too.

LEARN MORE

- *Difficult Conversations* by Douglas Stone, Bruce Patton and Sheila Heen of the Harvard Negotiation Project. This covers practical areas in a readable format for approaching difficult conversations, whether at work or at home.

A complete list of references can be found at the end of the book.

CHAPTER 7

HOW (AND WHY) TO SLEEP

Maria Kurtz is a hard-working head of school in a British university. She manages a large team of people and describes it as being like herding cats. She has put in many hours and much effort to get to the level she is at now. She has to her credit a degree, a PhD, numerous published articles, a co-edited book and many conference appearances. She manages a school with thousands of students, full and part time, from all over the world.

She also has two teenage children who are dealing with GCSEs and A levels, respectively. Her husband, Paul, is an accountant in a small firm in their local town.

This week she is feeling typically overstretched. But she is, as usual, coping without really being sure how. She starts the week – as usual – with a well-intentioned plan to get ahead. In order to do that, she goes through emails on Sunday night to pre-empt starting the week with some unexpected spanner in the works. Logging on at 9.30pm, she intends to be finished in half an hour but – again, not unusually – she gets sucked into answering some of the messages and ends up logging off just after 11pm. Her husband pours her a glass of wine from the bottle they opened earlier at dinner time, and she watches Desperate Housewives with him to wind down. By the time she turns her bedside light off it is 12.30am. She is briefly woken an hour later by her son clumping up the stairs to bed.

The working day starts early in the Kurtz household. The radio alarm springs into life at 6.30am and this morning is no exception. Maria and Paul's first experience of the day is speculation on how higher education is going to be affected by spending cuts. Paul gets up first, Maria hauls herself along to the bathroom after him but starts to feel fired up once she has her first coffee of the day. There is then the usual scramble to locate PE kit, front door keys and science books before they all head out in their respective directions.

Arriving at work, Maria turns on her computer and checks emails. Twenty new ones have arrived since turning it off last night. A couple of them are replies to messages she sent then. Half an hour later, a colleague drops in to discuss a problem he has with a student. This runs straight into a meeting at 10.30. Not yet on to her "to do" list for the day, she picks up the pile of marking she has to deal with and decides to spend the rest of the morning on that alone. Half way through marking the first one, the phone rings and she spends the rest of the morning (and lunch break) dealing with urgent requests for teaching figures that have just arrived.

By mid-afternoon, there is another meeting, this time with a PhD student she is supervising; a very enthusiastic and capable student whom she always enjoys meeting. The meeting goes on till 4.30pm. Turning back to her computer, she tackles the rest of the emails that have arrived during the afternoon. And then marks two more papers. Only 142 left to go. As Head of School she only has one module to mark, thankfully. By 6pm she is hungry and also conscious that she has promised her daughter to help her with some maths revision this evening. Getting home, she cooks pasta, eats quickly (the kids have already helped themselves to food earlier because they said they were too hungry to wait for her) and settles down to a fraught session with her daughter that ends with them shouting at each other, leaving both of them upset and mystified about how that happened. To calm down, they watch a bit of TV – whatever's on – it happens to be something about a family moving to Australia which is quite a nice diversion.

Once her husband gets home from a school governor's meeting at 9pm they stick to their New Year's resolution and take time out to have a glass of wine and a chat to each other about their respective days. Paul agrees to help her by listening to a run-through of the presentation she has put together for a big multi-institutional meeting she is going to on Thursday. The pressure is on as future funding may depend on making a good impression and a good case for the courses they are running. She runs through the presentation by 10.30pm and Paul's feedback is generally positive. He mentions that she may have made one or two slides too wordy but he doesn't think that's a big problem.

She stays up till 1.30am taking words out of the slides.

And a load out of the washing machine.

Going to bed immediately, she finds her head won't stop spinning and so she reads for an hour before finally dropping off.

The radio wakes them at 6.30am, this time with news of health care spending cuts.

What's happened to our sleep?

Sleep is usually one of the first things to be cut out when we are busy. On average some estimates say that we sleep an hour and a half less per night than the previous generation did in the 1950's. We all seem to still be managing so that's bought us an extra hour and a half per day to be productive, right? Well – maybe it's not that straightforward.

This chapter will look at the impact of letting our sleeping habits slide down to the bottom of the agenda. It will go on to suggest some ways in which we can improve the quality and quantity of our sleep, or to stop being as anxious about our sleep patterns as many people are.

The importance of sleep

A full explanation of why we sleep is, still, one of science's great unanswered questions. Research is clear, however, about some of the consequences of not getting enough sleep. Interestingly, many people in responsible jobs seem both able and willing to over-ride their need to sleep in pursuit of work goals and personal pleasure, heedless of those possible (and likely) consequences, some of which could even be deadly.

Brains need sleep to work at their best.

The fast paced, overloaded environment most people work in tends to make them ignore this sometimes mission-critical fact.

What do most senior managers' job specs look like?

The chances are, as a senior professional person in any organisation in the twenty first century, that the job spec is pretty vague and doesn't stand still long enough to completely pin it down. Many of the highly regarded and necessary skills needed now are more intangible; they are to do with communication and managing information. Things like these:

- Dealing with all sorts of novelty
- Comprehending and coping with a rapidly changing situation
- Remembering when events occurred
- Remembering very recent events

- Keeping track of events and updating the "big picture"
- Doing several things at once by remembering what you are doing, when to shift attention to another event and when to return back to the previous task
- Ignoring irrelevant information
- Changing plans in the light of new information
- Producing innovative solutions to problems
- Assessing risks and anticipating the range of consequences of an action
- Showing insight into one's own performance
- Having plenty of appropriate words to use for speaking
- Communicating effectively
- Controlling uninhibited behaviour such as irritable outbursts and losing one's temper
- Empathy with other people and detecting subtleties in their behaviour

Funny that. This list is actually taken from Jim Horne's book *Sleepfaring.* Jim is the Director of Loughborough University's Sleep Research Centre.

It is not a list of management job requirements. It is a list of the behaviours and skills lost with sleep deprivation.

The impact

Reflect on the last time you were involved in a project with major deadlines. I've witnessed enough (and sometimes done this myself) to know that sleep is often the first thing to be dismissed as the pizza orders go out and sleeves are rolled up for the evening.

Not only will everyone feel tired, which can sometimes be something of a badge of honour, but the chances are the project outcome is not as good as it ought to be, given the calibre of the people involved. It might be ok, it might be good.

Hopefully it won't include any catastrophic errors, although it is interesting to note that investigations into major industrial disasters often cite sleep depriving work patterns as a factor: the Space Shuttle disaster; Chernobyl; Three Mile Island to name a few. As for driving home afterwards – well, more on that later.

But the work quality probably isn't as good as it could be. It probably took longer and was more painful to achieve than it might have been. Given that a good result was the whole point of putting all the extra effort in, it's a bit of an own goal.

But I don't want to go to bed yet (or can't, I have too much to do)

Russell Foster, Professor of Circadian Neuroscience at Oxford University, also emphasises the critical role sleep plays in our cognitive functioning – in other words, the critical skills in all walks of life to be able to remember what's going on, to consolidate information, to make decisions, to learn new ways of doing things.

He reports studies that show the effect of chronic sleep deprivation over days on end was that

*"sleep loss caused a marked decline in waking performance, and, significantly, these individuals were **largely unaware of this deficit**"*

Well. There you have it really.

These hard working teams, toiling through the night, don't know that they are functioning less well than they could be. In fact, many work cultures reward *exactly the opposite* behaviour. The longer hours you work, the later you stay in the office, the more heroic your efforts to meet impossible deadlines – the more you will probably be perceived to be doing a great job.

In difficult economic times, it may seem as though there is really no alternative to working like this if you want to keep your job. The pressures are real. The example you may be set by your boss and colleagues may force you to adopt similar habits. The example we are all set by politicians working through the night and the apparent applause for those who seem not to need much sleep leads everyone to feel the pressure to ditch sleep and carry on.

But there are some good examples of people in very responsible positions who don't do this. Take some inspiration from the example of Winston Churchill, who was allegedly one of the world's great nappers. He always took a good hour and a half's nap in the afternoon and said it was the only way he could make good decisions.

He reportedly said "no half measures...get into bed. That's what I always do. Don't think you will be doing less work because you sleep during the day. That's a foolish notion held by people who have no imagination. You will be able to accomplish more."

The patterns of sleep vary between people – and depend upon opportunity (Winston was lucky in living above the shop I guess). But few organisations and leaders openly prioritise it as a very important part of performance.

Clearly the job entailed working some long hours (there was a war on after all). But if there was ever a time when leaders needed to be thinking clearly this must be one of them. I would like to think that our world leaders are following suit in recognising that sleep helps form good decisions. As well as the thousands of other people (ranging from my doctor to IT specialists to the school crossing lady) whose services I rely upon.

Tired? Or mildly depressed, anxious or generally out of sorts?

What a common cry it is to hear people say they are really tired. What do they actually mean?

"I could fall asleep anywhere" kind of tired

They may mean they are sleepy kind of tired. If this is the case, if they went to bed or laid down in a darkened room (or just sat quietly on a bus or in a cinema) they'd be drifting off. I can relate to that kind of tired. New parents can relate to that kind of tired. It probably indicates that they are not getting enough sleep. It's fairly straightforward, even if it's not always easy to fix in a busy lifestyle.

"I'm tired of all this" kind of tired

Tired can also mean bored, fed up or anxious; or indicate a desire to escape from the worries and concerns of the day. That retreat may well be a manifestation of the "fight or flight" response that can be triggered by perceived threats of whatever nature: redundancy; financial worries; health worries; that you can't find your keys (again).

This can lead on to –

Insomnia kind of tired

Disturbed sleep is closely linked to a range of mental health issues, and not just the serious, diagnosable ones. Most of us will be familiar with the early waking or difficulty falling or staying asleep when we are worried about something, or simply have a lot on our minds.

What can happen is that this leads to an obsession with the sleep itself so I have heard people tell me of ferocious attempts to cure themselves of insomnia ranging from drug treatment to complex bed time rituals to angrily pacing around mentally shouting at themselves and assuming they will never get a good night's sleep again. They add layers of worrying about being too tired the next day to their already fairly considerable list of worries. They may even be dwelling solely on worrying about lack of sleep.

Usually it is more effective in the longer term to focus on dealing with the things that might be keeping your mind on its race track. It is advisable to deal with them during the day, not in the middle of the night.

Meditation, exercise, and calming bedtime routines can help but are still attempting to sooth a troubled mind rather than dealing with root causes. Stress management is nearly always a mix of changing something about the cause of the stress as well as building resources to cope with challenging situations.

Having said that, there is great scope for anxiety-provoked wakefulness to become a vicious circle, so that the sleep quality itself becomes a source of anxiety. As far as possible, try to accept that your sleep is disturbed rather than becoming furious and wound up about it. I know it's much easier said than done. It's a good approach to spend some time in the day time addressing the causes of any anxiety if you can.

There are no universal cures for insomnia and most people will experience spells of it but it will pass when life moves on to another phase. There are a great many tempting "miracle cures" out there but I would recommend sticking to the research findings even though they might not be as seductive or promise as much. If you find something harmless that can harness the placebo effect though, it may not be something you want to sneeze at.

A note of warning – I am not covering sleep disorders such as sleep apnoea in this chapter. I am also not covering other possible health causes of uncharacteristic tiredness. If you feel excessively tired or sleepy or both, you should always consult your doctor.

What can you do about improving sleep?

Do you want to improve it?

No?

If you don't believe sleep is important enough, then there's probably not much point in sitting through lectures on it: whether from me, your partner, your mother or world renowned academics. That seems to be the issue in many work cultures. If the deadline or late night TV programme or siren call of emails and Facebook is more pressing in your opinion, then nothing is likely to change your mind.

I want to get better sleep when I think about it during the day or when wrenching myself out of bed in the morning but by bed time I want to stay up

This is at the heart of so many of our lifestyle choices, whether to do with food, sleep, exercise, homework, or the whole gamut of self improvement or healthy living.

What is going on is the old chestnut of balancing instant gratification with delayed rewards. The reward for early nights comes later in the week or month when you are more on the ball at work perhaps, or can enjoy a film or conversation in a more satisfying way.

But the instant gratification is another cup of tea and an episode of your favourite vice on the telly. Or it may be work related in the belief that you can get ahead by being on email at odd hours. Of course you're probably tired so giving in to the immediate temptation is easier than summoning the energy to get up and go to bed.

The same dilemma is present in every diet and every attempt to get fitter or to give up smoking. In the immediate moment, the options are all the nice things: easier, more attractive, tastier, more relaxing, warmer, drier, maybe even a bit rebellious or naughty.

Longer term the damage that giving in to the instant gratification becomes apparent: being knackered, unfit and fat (to be blunt).

There is no easy quick fix. You have to want to change and be convinced of the benefits of that change. Habits can take weeks to change and other people can't do it for you, even though they can help and support very effectively.

I really do want to improve my sleep

OK. This is when you are ready to put some effort into establishing new habits, rediscovering old ones, or strengthening those you already have.

Ten top tips for increasing the chances of a good night's sleep

This is mainly about having restful routines that help you to manage the spill-over of the day's work into your sleep time. It's not rocket science but it is amazing how casually many of us treat these things as if they just don't matter, or don't affect us. Nurture lovely associations in your bedroom: quiet, calm, relaxing, a true retreat.

1. Don't have lots of stimulating, light emitting things going on in the bedroom – TV, computer, phones, fancy alarm systems and so on. **Keep it dark and quiet.**

2. **Keep the room cool, but yourself warm.** Warm hands and feet are important. Sleep is triggered by a fall in body temperature as you relax; a warm bath before bed can help that by temporarily raising your body temperature and allowing it to drop once you are in bed.

3. **Don't drink caffeine close to bed time.** Different people have different sensitivities to caffeine and it can be very useful in providing a bit of a boost when you need it (see driving below, for example), but be careful and experiment with when your last strong coffee of the day should be.

4. **Don't rely on alcohol to send you off to sleep.** It will. But you will wake up later feeling a bit groggy and then are more likely to get into a cycle of using one thing to send you to sleep and another to wake you up and that just messes with what your body wants to do.

5. **Go with it if you are a lark or an owl** – there seems to be some genetic difference between people (and it is also possibly to be somewhere in between) so some will naturally prefer early nights and mornings and others won't. It can be a bit of an issue depending on your job (or your partner!) of course, but as far as you can, fall into line with your natural tendencies.

6. **Don't work in bed.** Don't have any work triggers in the bed room if you can help it. Work is in one place and bed in another. This is much more restful and helps to prevent work related thoughts getting into bed with you.

7. **Don't obsess with what the time is whilst in bed.** If you wake up or have to get up try not to look at the clock. Set your alarm and put it out of reach. It makes it easier to get

back to sleep, as noticing the time often sets off an anxious and irritated set of responses and in many ways it really doesn't matter what the time is.

8. In societies where there is no artificial light, people behave in calm, quiet ways for around two hours at dusk. This is a **natural wind down period**, which many of us will replicate for our young children even in our twenty four hour society. But once those children hit their teens, and adulthood, it seems that wind down stage often gets ditched, for them and for us. Lots of us work, watch stimulating programmes, do domestic chores, argue, surf the internet, eat and drink and so on late into the evening. We then expect to just switch off instantly to go to sleep. It's too big an ask for most bodies and minds.

9. If you can't sleep, Jim Horne recommends that you **don't beat yourself up** trying but get up, go to another room and do something bland but engaging. He suggests jigsaws. It could equally be knitting, playing patience, making models, those kind of things. It shouldn't be something hugely physical, or passive like watching TV. And ideally should not involve caffeinated drinks. Stay well away from work or emails or the like. It feels ridiculous but you're awake anyway. Do this until you start to feel sleepy then go back to bed, turn the light off, and snuggle down. If you're not asleep fairly soon but feel yourself getting more awake, just get up and repeat the process. It doesn't matter if this goes on all night. Get up at your usual time, get through the day (try not to sleep during the day, and make sure you get outside for a good dose of natural light), and start again the next night. Over time this process should reduce the anxiety and also bring the routine back. Whether you realise it or not, you will be getting enough

sleep to function in this way, it's just that it feels very uncomfortable.

10. Try to remember that you are not different from everyone else. Whilst you have probably been managing (well) on little or disturbed sleep, you could find you are much more efficient in all areas of your life if you change one or two aspects of your sleep time. Try it and see!

Beware

There are two key areas where people may be especially vulnerable if they have lost sleep: driving and jet lag. This can lead us to being so vulnerable that the chances of being killed by sleep loss are much higher than people realise. These points cannot be overemphasised for the huge numbers of working people who are regularly travelling across time zones and driving long distances to meetings.

Driving

Driving to meetings is so common that most of us don't give it a second thought. The dangers of driving when you are sleepy are severe. But nearly everyone asked about it will vehemently deny that they are taking risks in this way.

Sleep related crashes are most likely on monotonous roads, at speed (typically on motorways) and between 2am and 6am, or early afternoon, when the body clock makes most of us feel sleepier than the rest of the time. There are usually no skid marks, which is one sign to investigators that the driver fell asleep. A micro sleep of around seven seconds is obviously enough for the (possibly fatal) damage to be done. For drivers who survive these kinds of crashes, they usually will deny having fallen asleep. This is because if you are woken up within two minutes of falling asleep you usually don't realise you have been asleep at all. A driver is unlikely to manage more than two minutes of sleep before hitting something (or someone).

This is scary stuff, not only for sleepy drivers taking these risks but for the rest of us on the road. So what should you do?

....

What to do if you are sleepy when driving

- **ADMIT** to yourself that you are sleepy. Drivers hardly ever fall asleep without warning. They knew they were feeling sleepy. They just pretended they weren't.
- **REMIND** yourself just how dangerous this is. The effect is easily the same as being over the legal alcohol level, often worse. What about your family, your colleagues, your reputation and other road users if you fall asleep?
- **DO NOT** rely on strategies like opening the window, turning the music up. If you are fighting off sleep in this way you are at a very dangerous stage.
- **THE BEST ADVICE** from the experts in the field is to pull over, have a coffee, then set an alarm and have a nap of up to 20 minutes (no more). Do this in this order. The caffeine will give you a boost but takes about twenty minutes to kick in. The nap will deal with the sleepiness whilst the caffeine takes effect. Other ideas such as walking around for some fresh air will wake you up in the short term but a few miles down the road you are likely to be just as sleepy again.
- You may feel stupid, or worried about being late, but really – **LATE OR DEAD? LATE OR IN A LONG EXPENSIVE SHAMEFUL COURT CASE** because you have killed someone else? Communicate with people over how your

journey is going, and manage their expectations if you are experiencing problems.

(Taken from *Sleepfaring* by Jim Horne – a good read for more on the topic of sleep and safety.)

....

If you are a manager of other people

If you are a manager of other people you owe it to them to alert them to the dangers, to model safe behaviour in this respect and to give them permission to deal with their sleepiness safely. It is a massively under-discussed area. Your staff may be dismissed if they were caught drink driving. Driving whilst sleepy is just as dangerous, and is actually just as irresponsible.

Keep in mind what is expected of yourself and your staff. I know of people who regularly go on work trips abroad, involving crossing several time zones and a hectic schedule, who then arrive back at Heathrow in the early hours and immediately jump in the car to drive for hours up the motorway. There must be a better way. Can you as a manager influence at least what you and your staff do even if you can't change the organisation?

Jet lag

If you are crossing time zones, you will of course be vulnerable to jet lag, which is when your body clock is struggling to adapt to the new situation it finds itself in. Some people seem to suffer more from this than others, and it can vary depending on what direction you are travelling in. Generally it is easier to travel westwards (from the UK to the USA for example) than the other way around. Travelling westwards will involve staying up later than your body might want to until it gets to a reasonable bed time whereas eastwards involves going to bed before your body clock wants to which is generally a trickier proposition.

I heard of one person, a senior academic, who travelled a lot with his job and on one occasion rang his secretary from a foreign train station platform in a completely disorientated state. He had travelled across various time zones by then in a short succession of time and by then had no idea where he was or what he was supposed to be doing next.

I met another who had a crazy global marketing role that meant he averaged ten hours a week of sleep. When I met him, he was no longer in that job. He had had a breakdown and had to leave. This is fortunately relatively rare, but feels as if it should be avoidable.

How can you deal with the effects of jet lag?

The main suggestions are:
- **The importance of natural light** – this is the biggest influence on our body clocks. It is many times brighter than the brightest artificial lights even on a cloudy day. Professor Russell Foster (Chair of Circadian Neuroscience at Oxford University) has discovered that there are light receptors in the eye which are dedicated to using light to influence the body clock. This means that you can be visually blind but natural light is still important in timing your sleep and wakefulness.

  So, when travelling across time zones, make a real effort to get outside in the late morning/midday when the light is brightest for at least half an hour. Suggest you talk whilst going for a walk if you are in back to back meetings, and explain why you will be more effective for the whole visit if you do that. It is also worth bearing this in mind in your day to day work, especially in the winter time; many of us never see natural daylight in a normal working day and it can make it much more difficult to have regular sleep patterns.

- **Don't use melatonin** unless your doctor prescribes it. Some people have found it to be helpful but if you do take it be careful when to take it as you risk interfering further with the body clock in the longer term.
- **Don't use sleeping tablets** unless prescribed either. Again, these artificial means of getting to sleep can have their uses but generally will exacerbate problems in terms of moving away further from a natural regulation of sleep and wakefulness.
- **Try to stick to local going to bed and getting up times** – if you are travelling west (eg. UK to USA), this means staying up later than your body clock wants to. Have a coffee, a walk outside and try to keep going until you are within range of a normal bed time (9.30 or so). If travelling east, and especially if this involves an overnight flight which is common from USA to UK, allow yourself up to two hours sleep when you are craving to crash out but limit it to that. Then again, get daylight, and have a coffee, and aim to keep going until it gets to a local bed time.

Good night, sleep tight

Sleep is free, pleasant, side-effect free, and essential to brain functioning. It makes you better at whatever it is you choose to do in your waking time. It should be a guilt free pleasure. Enjoy!

CHAPTER SEVEN – IN BRIEF

- Sleep is easily dismissed but essential for good functioning, especially elements of good decision-making.
- Often sleep gets postponed or ignored in favour of more instant gratification such as late night television, surfing the internet or trying to get ahead on work related emails.
- In some areas such as driving behaviour and jet lag, lack of sleep can be dangerous. But in most cases, it just means that we're not as alert or full of life as we could be, which makes a busy life feel like harder work than ever.

LEARN MORE

- *Counting Sheep: the science and pleasures of sleep and dreams* by Paul Martin. This is a highly entertaining and well-researched book.
- *Sleep: a very short introduction* by Russell Foster and Steven Lockley. This book is going to be published at the end of 2011, and is one of the Oxford University Press's *Very Short Introductions* series. I have spoken to Russell about this book whilst it was in progress, and I am very much looking forward to reading it. It's likely to be a well-informed and speedy way into the subject, given the nature of this series of short books.
- *Sleepfaring: a journey through the science of sleep* by Jim Horne, of the Loughborough University Sleep Research Centre. Jim is an interesting speaker in this area too.
- *The Rhythms of Life: the biological clocks that control the daily lives of every living thing* by Leon Kreitzman and

Russell Foster – for more depth on the fascinating subject of biological clocks.

- www.howdidyousleep.org This website is part of the Mental Health Foundation's 2011 campaign, following publication of their report *Sleep Matters*. The website has downloadable resources including the report itself and a sleep relaxation MP3.

A complete list of references can be found at the end of the book.

CHAPTER 8

EXERCISE

"Adults should do a minimum of 30 minutes moderate-intensity physical activity, at least five days a week. For children and young people, the target is at least 60 minutes a day."
—UK Government Advice, 2011

This is going to be a relatively short chapter.

It surely must be impossible to be the sort of person who is reading this book and to not know that exercise is good for you.

Exercise is critical in mental and physical health and is implicated in just about every element of health that you can think of, ranging from Alzheimer's to heart disease to depression to obscure disorders you have probably never heard of.

Why don't we do enough of it then?

Exercise is also the one thing that usually gets knocked off our agendas first. This is because:
- We don't think we've got time
- We feel too tired
- Exercise is painful/unpleasant/cold/humiliating
- It's not as urgent as other things in our day

I am familiar with all of this.

And so, it would seem, are lots of other people. I did a straw poll survey of busy, professional, working people. Here are some of the things they said:

The barriers

I think we often feel least like doing it at times when we'd benefit most. eg when stressed or being very busy at work absorbs energy in other ways. Also, as I get older, if I do a lot more than usual (or haven't done a form of exercise for a long time), I find I get more severe reactions after- particularly aching arms/shoulders. This puts me off, although I know doing some more (but maybe more gently) would help.
—University teacher, UK

It's easier to sit/ lay down than be more active
—Small business owner

Lately I have been so tired from stressful days at work I feel mentally and physically drained. A meal out/TV with a glass of wine requires nothing mental/physical
—Senior manager, University

We have a tendency to pursue things that give us immediate gratification. The long-term health benefits of exercise are not as tantalizing as curling up with a glass of wine and a good book.
—University professor, Maryland

I think people forget how good exercise makes them feel. Once they become unfit it is initially hard to get going due to the effort required.
—Managing Director, Xchanging Procurement Services

Pressure from girlfriend to stay home and watch TV with her, having plans with friends and being tired are the 3 most common things to stop me visiting the gym
—IT security consultant

Right now I have other priorities: looking after my children & pets, doing my PhD, earning money, keeping the house and garden habitable and spending a bit of time each day doing something I find fun. These things shouldn't really come before my personal health and fitness, but they do. I ought to re-categorise exercise as 'fun' but I'd be lying to myself if I pretended it was.
—Freelance writer/editor and PhD student

Perhaps it's the feeling that we need to be fit to do exercise otherwise it's not very enjoyable and it takes a lot of effort to get to that stage. Most exercise is exercise for its own sake rather than something enjoyable in itself or that can be incorporated into another part of our lives e.g. cycling to work or running round the park with the children or playing tennis
—Partner, London law firm

On a recent walk in Derbyshire (an activity I would generally say I'm very enthusiastic about), I tried to work out what was going on. I came to the conclusion that I don't actually like the physical sensations associated with real exertion: hurting muscles; pounding heart; overheating; sweaty skin and damp clothes; a dry mouth; a runny nose in cold air. It's all a bit like having the flu.

This was all happening as we toiled up a steep hill.

Once at the top, however, it was a different story. Breath back, pulse back to normal, I then loved the even warmth from a good blood flow; a cool breeze on my face was very welcome; the view was uplifting; muscles felt positively zinging. And later in the day, once we were back at home, showered and changed, we ate and slept like kings.

As with so many other things, it's another instance of delayed gratification.

What the people who love exercise say

I know there are people for whom there appears not to be much of a physical or psychological pain barrier to get them up and out there and doing enough to keep them in tip top condition. The survey revealed some of this persuasion:

You will always find the time to do something you like – what you need to do is find a form of exercise you enjoy. Normally get out on my bike for 2 hours at 6.30am on Sat / Sun – home by the time everyone else is getting up.
—Martin, an accountant in Ireland

I prefer to be active and outside rather than sitting in a chair watching TV especially during the summer time. I even enjoy active holidays e.g. walking/trekking, skiing, sailing etc.!!!
—Curriculum manager, training provider

Is exercise good for health? yes – as a scientist I have read all the evidence and am totally convinced. Why do I do it? – a mix of (a) the above and (b) fortunate to have found activities I love doing (c) have a sporty partner – so much so I don't call them exercise - e.g. orienteering
—Catherine Hughes, Health and fitness consultant

Not only do I enjoy it and feel better physically, but also it's the best stress relief that I know. It's also sort of an addiction for me (if I cannot work out two days in a row then I've got a problem) —Senior manager B4 firm

Talking in a little more detail with some people who think like this, they can sometimes vaguely remember a time when the off-putting physical sensations were just that – off-putting. It seems they have done enough exercise, frequently enough, to forget this though. Their minds and bodies are now in a state of wanting to be active, and being very aware of missing it if circumstances prevent them running or whatever their thing is.

Perhaps it's all to do with endorphins (which could usefully kick in a bit more sharply in my experience).

Whatever it is, many of us find it difficult to get to a point where exercise is as much part of our daily or weekly lives as eating our dinner or brushing our teeth.

How many of us don't seem to have a natural exercise bent?

30% of the people who answered my survey (54 professional people) said that they had good intentions about exercise but it dropped off the agenda. Even the much bigger group (60%) who said they enjoyed it and looked forward to it, very often found other things got in the way.

The average number of hours spent exercising a week was 5.5, whereas the very honest admission of how many hours on average were spent in sedentary leisure such as television, internet and reading was 17.5 hours a week.

The Office for National Statistics (ONS) published figures in 2011 which indicated that watching television was the most common leisure activity for nearly 90% of adults. On average, in 2010, adults in the UK spent 3.5 hours a day watching television; 2.5 hours a day on the computer; and an hour listening to the radio.

Just over 50% of adults had taken part in any form of sport or exercise in the four weeks prior to the survey. The most common reason given for not doing any, or enough, was lack of time.

You can draw your own conclusions from these statistics. I would venture that lack of time, whilst sometimes a real constraint, is more often a bit of an excuse. It would seem we don't lack time to watch television or surf the internet.

We could quote figures from endless surveys all day. This would probably act as a good way of procrastinating and distracting rather than actually doing any exercise. So let's get moving.

Finding your get up and go (before it's got up and gone)

The benefits

It can really help to remember the benefits of being active as something of a carrot rather than stick. The cardiovascular and mental health benefits of exercise start pretty much as soon as you get out of your chair, which is worth knowing and reminding yourself about.

It seems to me to be a small flaw in the design of the human body that you can't really experience good cardiovascular health in a very immediate way. You can't see or feel your heart, lungs or circulation until they go wrong (often suddenly and drastically). But knowing that those benefits are building with every step you take can help to make it feel worthwhile to be active.

Other, possibly more noticeable, benefits were covered by my survey respondents:

- *Walking makes me feel ready for work in the morning, after a stressful day at work the 30 minute walk home gives me time to calm down.* (Assistant Consultant URS/Scott Wilson)
- *Increased energy; better outlook on life; feel healthier* (Accountant)
- *I can eat well, helps me sleep. The dog is happy and tired.* (Clinical psychologist)
- *Feeling better. Also, personal appearance is very important for my business. Was overweight as a child/teenager and in my early 20's. I work hard to make sure I maintain my fitness levels. It gives me more confidence and it is part of my daily routine.* (Director)
- *Fitness, flexibility, clearer head for problem-solving* (freelance editor)
- *It's an opportunity to switch off from things. When I run or cycle I don't think about anything else.* (IT analyst)
- *Dissipates frustration, invigorates, and helps offset my enjoyment of food* (architect)
- *Feeling more awake, improved physical and mental capability, relieve stress, social interaction, break from work* (MBA student)
- *Exercising is good for my brain, I can reflect properly on things. I can feel my body being put to good use i.e my muscles ache afterwards.* (lawyer)
- *Stronger, less pain, improved mood, connecting with people and nature* (small business owner)
- *Reflection on work/life. Camaraderie. Good health.* (head teacher)
- *For me it is absolutely necessary. Having a myocardial infarction at the age of 31, I have no choice about exercise*

to keep the heart pumping. (QA specialist in HE, Abu Dhabi)

We mostly know all this. But it's good to be reminded.

Just do it – overcoming the barriers

Prioritising

Exercise can easily fall off the agenda if it is there in the first place as "something I'll do when I've got time". You probably won't have time. Suggestions are:

- Do exercise first. Make the other stuff fit around the exercise rather than vice versa.
- Book in at a class or session or with a team or club – so you have a commitment which is on a par with any other meeting or commitment.
- Sign up to a race or event that requires training to lead up to it. It can legitimise the time spent exercising as well as motivate you to do it.

"Set specific goals to provide reason to do the exercise, timetabling the exercise into a normal day, ensuring that exercise is given as high a priority as work and rest, drinking & eating correctly especially in the periods immediately before exercise" (MBA student)

Mindgames

People have all sorts of ways of tricking themselves into thinking positively about exercise. Here are some of the particularly imaginative (and you can copy them, and add to them. I am.):

- Time spent walking or cycling to work is gained time. For example, if you cycle for an hour to work, but it would have taken you half an hour to drive, this has replaced the driving time with exercise which would otherwise need to be done in addition to the driving time. This has therefore woven an extra half hour into your day (I know, this takes a bit of a mind shift!).
- Keep your mind on how you will feel afterwards.
- Don't let yourself ask questions like "is today the best day or would it be better to go tomorrow?" Squash that with whatever version of "just do it" works for you.
- Seeing exercise as a remedy for feeling tired rather than tired being a reason not to do exercise.
- Viewing aching muscles as a good sign of beneficial activity, not pain to avoid.
- Exercise will save time in the longer term as it will mean you are faster at the jobs you have to do because you are rested, fitter and clearer mentally.
- Don't call it exercise. Call it something more inviting – "fun" perhaps. If that's stretching a point, try something in between – "benefit", "health enhancer", "energy boost".
- Read up on the health benefits and science – keep a note of three facts that are most compelling from your perspective.

"Seeing exercise as part of my day. I know how important it is to my business so I actually see it as part of my marketing strategy" (Director, retail business)

Health scares
Sadly this often does provide a wakeup call for many and exercise is then prioritised pretty efficiently. Suddenly we can find time.

- Physical or mental health scares can provide the impetus. The survey included people with injury, heart problems, anxiety and depression, as well as longer term physical illnesses. Exercise can help recovery from all of these. Exercise can also help to prevent them in the first place. If possible, learn from others on this and don't let it be your own scare that sends you for your trainers.
- Learn more about what physical sensations you should watch for. It can be difficult to assess whether pain in any part of your body is a reason to stop exercising or whether it is a sign that you need to do more until you are fitter. Especially if you have reason to be concerned about your health, it is well worth getting some informed help about this, whether from physiotherapists, your doctor or reputable fitness instructors.

A few quotes speak volumes here:
Watching the ill-effects of sedentary life styles on the internet and on the television is motivating (associate Abacus Consulting)

Health fright - do or die - accepting that walking costs nothing and I don't need any fancy kit or expense (University public relations manager)

I was very fit, energetic and toned before I became ill. I know that the only way to be fit again in the future is to just get on with it - on a regular and frequent basis. It's mind over matter really. No one else can make my body fit! (retired University lecturer)

A few years ago I experienced serious anxiety and it made me aware of how important exercise is to my welfare (former public sector manager)

Other people

As with so many areas in life, the support and encouragement of others can be massively powerful. Equally, the disapproval or mockery from others is just as influential in the other direction.

- **Enlist the encouraging people** – those who will spur you on without making you feel bad for not keeping up. Find friends or instructors/leaders/coaches for activities who will help you to feel good in your endeavours. At whatever level.
- **Use the competitive spirit carefully** – it can work wonders for some and be completely off-putting for others to be measured against yourself or others. You know what is most likely to be motivating but not overwhelming for you. It won't necessarily be the same for other people you know. Use it – but use it well and in your own interests.
- **Keep the doubting people in their place** – people have all sorts of reasons to stop you doing exercise. It might make them feel guilty if you do and they don't. They might want you to keep them company on the sofa. They might feel fearful of the impact of exercise on you (and them). They might pour scorn on your efforts. Give the encouraging people more air time, and try to turn the volume down from the doubters. There's no science in this but how about having two encouraging people on your side for every one who is trying to tempt you away from becoming more active? You might end up convincing the doubters to join you in due course.
- **Learn** – from books, websites, television, other people. There are plenty of examples and stories out there from other people who have overcome adversity, or taken up various sports, or can inspire you to get moving. Model yourself on them.

- **Yourself** – just a note that very often we are our own harshest critics and give ourselves such a beating up for not doing as much as we intended or as much as other people (or for not being as good at something as we would like), that it's no wonder another part of us rebels and refuses to change into our gym kit.

Go gently with yourself. Targets and goals can be great – but don't tear into yourself if you miss a training session. Bring yourself back to it gently. It's not about making excuses but about accepting that life is often complex and our motivations not always clear even to ourselves.

If you fall off the wagon, just gather yourself and get back on. Don't throw yourself under the wheels.

And a final point

What you choose to do in terms of exercise tends to be not as important as doing *something*.

Here's a little taster – the full range of activities mentioned in my survey. It might give you a couple of ideas. They all come from people with pretty packed schedules.

Aerobics / Athletics / Badminton / Circuit training / Cycling / Dance / Dog walking / Elliptical trainer / Five-a-side football / Flexibility exercises / Gardening / Golf / Gym / Hill walking / Hockey / Housework / Ice hockey / Martial arts / Nordic walking / Orienteering / Pilates / Power lifting / Rock climbing / Rowing / Running / Skating / Soccer with the kids / Spinning / Stability ball / Step aerobics / Swimming / Tai Chi / Tennis / Treadmill / Walking to work / Water aerobics / Wii / Yoga

CHAPTER EIGHT – IN BRIEF

- Exercise has mental health as well as physical health benefits. You probably already know that. This chapter focuses on what might stop us doing exercise even so.
- Challenge the most common reason given for not doing exercise – there isn't time.
- Anything is better than nothing. It's important to identify and overcome the barriers to exercise. Easier said than done but it *is* possible.

LEARN MORE

- *How to look after your mental health using exercise* – a free downloadable report from the Mental Health Foundation (www.mentalhealth.org.uk).
- *Keep your heart healthy* – a downloadable booklet from the British Heart Foundation (www.bhf.org.uk). Whilst this does of course focus on cardiovascular health, all the same things apply to mental well-being too when it comes to exercise. And getting some facts about the physical benefits of exercise can help to motivate us to do exercise in the first place.
- *Fit for over-40's for Dummies* by Betsy Nagelsen McCormack and Mike Yorkey – I realise this may be insulting some readers, wrapping both over 40 and dummies into the same reference. But I personally think the *Dummies* series of books is pretty good, at least at a taster level to get you started. You don't have to read it!

A complete list of references can be found at the end of the book.

CHAPTER 9

WORKING LUNCH

"It is more fun to talk with someone who doesn't use long, difficult words but rather short, easy words like "What about lunch?""
—Winnie the Pooh, AA Milne

Is lunchtime endangered?

We work in an era of huge information and opportunity. There is probably more choice and availability of great food for lunch when we are at work than there has ever been. Most of us are well aware that fruit and vegetables are good for us. That too much saturated fat and salt isn't. That drinking alcohol at lunchtime doesn't usually improve the afternoon's output.

We know and act on some of the good advice that is so readily available. But if there was ever an area of our daily lives that is subject to peer pressure, throughout our lives, it seems that it is what you do with your lunch break.

The food we consume is one thing (a very important thing); but are our lunching habits helping us do a good job or feel well?

I carried out a small survey to find out more. I asked:

Have your lunchtime habits changed over your working life?

- *Definitely. The more senior role I have held the less time I have felt able to take for lunch. Also – availability of laptop and blackberry mean I feel as though I constantly need to work through lunch* (senior manager in charity)
- *I work from home with a colleague who always goes out for lunch so I tend to stay in. If anything I make more effort not to work through lunch than previously* (graphic designer in small creative agency)
- *Generally never have had time for dedicated lunch throughout school career* (headteacher)
- *I eat on the go now or eat while driving. Ten years ago I would sit for at least half an hour and enjoy what I was eating* (on site massage therapist, mature student and mother of three)
- *I suspect that as my jobs have become more "serious" my lunch breaks have shortened. Many years ago I worked in a call centre and I always took lunch breaks and read a book. In my previous job I worked in a very small team and we always ate lunch together and did the crossword which did wonders for morale. These days I rarely take time out to have lunch* (anonymous)
- *Lunch breaks have always been short – 30 mins max – but when on site in my earlier years there would be some time to relax with colleagues too* (managing director of an SME construction company)
- *Today, read the trade press. Other days, lunch is with colleagues, business contacts or with friends. Some weeks, we have team meetings or seminars. So, no two lunch hours are the same! Sometimes, if I have a deadline I have*

to work right through lunch without eating anything at all.
(senior lawyer, international law firm, Brussels)

- *Back in the late 80's I would take an hour for lunch. I always went out for a walk and would return to eat with my colleagues. Now I still try to have 30 minutes but even feel a little guilty at this amount of time. I try to encourage my team to take a break at lunchtime as I believe it makes them more productive and focused in the afternoon* (managing director in marketing agency)

- *Very recently I have made a concerted effort to get away from my desk at least twice a week. Prior to that I had no break at all (and that has gone on for a number of years)* (senior manager at a university)

- *1980's: at least one day a week to pub, rest of time shop bought sandwiches 1990's: at least one day a week to restaurant / cafe, rest of time shop bought sandwiches 2000's: shop bought sandwiches at desk 2010's: home-made sandwiches at desk. Guess it reflects my perceived (rise and fall in) wealth, rise of internet, health, changes in office location* (senior structural engineer)

- *As I got more senior roles it was easier to just keep going over the lunch time at my desk* (global HR business partner in market research)

- *I go out far less to avoid eating large lunches in a restaurant* (consulting actuary)

- *I rarely take lunch breaks. Once a week at most I take more than half an hour. Most lunch breaks are eating at my desk, doing work or personal activities. I wish I could do fitness activity in my lunch hours but my workload is now far too great to spare the time. Nobody is stopping me from taking lunch breaks but I feel compelled by the scale of my workload.* (University public relations)

The food

The food itself is only part of the story. Of the responses I
got from my survey, as well as thinking about what coaching
clients have told me, most people at middle and senior levels
in organisations eat reasonably good food: salads, soups,
sandwiches, fruit, with the odd chocolate bar or packet of crisps
thrown in. The extremes on my survey went from "Very little
– because lunch is on the hoof – maybe a banana" through to
"salad, stuffed vine leaves, hummus, crisps, clementine, figs and
mozzarella".

It's probably a self-selecting group. These are (by and large)
people who are well-educated and hold demanding senior
positions. Their organisations often facilitate the provision of
good quality food either by their location in city centres or by
having good canteens or sandwich deliveries. I suspect wider
patterns amongst the whole population are not as good.

There is a huge amount of misleading, contradictory and
fad-driven information around in relation to food and diets as
any browse of the internet or book shop will tell you.

However, there is very good advice in amongst that too, and
one of the best authors I have come across for sound advice and
information about nutrition is Jane Clarke. As a state registered
dietician here in the UK, she is experienced about advising on
the relationship between food and health (both physical and
mental) based on solid evidence. She also has a real feel for how
enjoyable food can be. No hair shirt or wacky approaches to
food in her books, which makes me a big fan. Food can be a
daily delight.

In *Body Foods for Life*, she writes, "Despite the tremendous
pressures of today's society, we all need to take regular
replenishing breaks and find stress-relieving activities. We also

need to make sure our body receives the nutrients it needs. If we try to cheat our body by cutting corners, it will eventually falter. As tempting as it is to miss breakfast or keep going until late in the office without eating anything, or expect the body to respond well to chocolate bars and endless cups of coffee, these will not bring you health and happiness."

Or, I would add, will they bring you sustainable work related performance. Whatever it might feel like, the chances are you will be doing a better long term job if you eat well.

The drink

What we drink can be an unconscious habit. Water, caffeine and alcohol are a major part of many of our routines. It is easy to forget how they might be affecting the energy we have for our work (and anything else).

I am not going to start advocating abstinence from alcohol and caffeine. As you may have picked up already, I enjoy a good coffee and the same goes for a well-timed glass of wine.

It's just worth reviewing your habits every now and then. Are they working for or against you?

Whilst it would seem that drinking alcohol at lunchtime may have declined, it's very easy to end up drinking quite a lot at home, especially if times are stressful. This is not an uncommon story in the people I have coached, and is a trend backed up by the most recent report by the Office for National Statistics on the topic (*Smoking and drinking among adults, 2009*).

They found that average weekly alcohol consumption was highest in the managerial and professional group and lowest amongst those in routine or manual jobs. The groups with the highest household income drank the most. This applies to men and women but is particularly pronounced for women in managerial and professional jobs. Sobering statistics. Or possibly not.

I think worth a second thought though.

The time

In my snapshot, the average length of lunch break came in at 28 minutes. Over ten per cent of my sample of sixty six professional people just worked through, eating (or not) whilst they work.

A bigger survey carried out for the Chartered Society of Physiotherapy in the UK in 2010 found an even higher number, one in three, people work through their lunch break, with one in four taking no break at all during the day. Nearly half of the people surveyed then go on to say that their physical pains are due to working in the same position for a long time. Hmmm.

It is no surprise that the time feels so pressured. It is pressured. I am yet to meet many people who don't have more than enough to do in the time they have available.

So what do people do with the 28 minutes they might take as a break?

Well, about a third of my respondents surfed the internet, social media or emails. Slightly fewer than that went out for a walk; some watched the news or chatted to colleagues. One went swimming, one had a coffee with a friend and one walked the dog. Two, working from home, dealt with washing and domestic chores (I didn't take part, it wasn't me).

It appears that nothing very dramatic happens in most of our lunchtimes.

We get food, we eat it. We might pause briefly to see what our friends, family, the weather or the world is up to.

Then we press on.

The company

Two thirds of my survey sample spent their lunch break alone. This was sometimes a deliberate policy (*"I sit in the park to avoid people if I get the chance and the weather is nice"*) otherwise it just happened that way. There are, of course, pros and cons to spending that time with others or spending it alone; and different people will have different preferences. One is not, of itself, better or worse than the other.

But it might reflect some of the issues raised in the chapter about other people. Does this often solitary desk-based lunch time mean that we are missing out on a sense of being part of something? Does it mean we are missing out on the informal conversations with colleagues that might actually be extremely useful in doing a good job? And does it mean we are missing a laugh or a shoulder to cry on about things that go on at work?

Food for thought: the hospital doctor

One senior hospital consultant told me that when he started out, the lunch break was sacrosanct for senior consultants. It was held in a formal dining room with good food and all the trappings of a formidable hierarchy which was not always helpful.

What it did provide however, was a point in the day when consultants could chat with colleagues they rarely crossed paths with in the course of a working day, as they were holed up in their own operating theatres and surgeries, or who may work in a different discipline. The informal discussion of hot topics in their practice often was a short cut to new alliances and development of new techniques. I could also be a good way of mentoring more junior doctors as they were admitted to the lunchtime inner sanctum.

This same doctor, now in the senior position himself, rarely had time to grab a sandwich at his desk, let alone sit with an after dinner coffee and chew over the events of the morning with other experienced colleagues.

There were undoubtedly things about the old system that were exclusive and possibly even unfair, but without any chance of a relaxed exchange of ideas as they arise, it's likely that we all work harder in a more isolated way. How many of us are busily re-inventing the wheel when if we only chatted to the person working in the next team to us, we might find the answer straight away?

I am wary of drawing "good old days" conclusions. But some of the reflections I've heard would suggest that not everyone feels refreshed or motivated by a lonesome refuelling in front of the computer. That wasn't even an option a generation ago.

The peer pressure (aka the work culture)

I believe that this is the biggest influence. It applies to much more than just lunch breaks of course.

Meals are a particularly interesting social phenomenon. On the face of it, we need only shove down enough calories and nutrients to keep our bodies working. People have rarely treated food as unemotionally as that though.

Meals can be good or bad: celebratory blow-outs, high art, a power game, a bonding ritual, an adventure, a comfort, a source of social anxiety, or a form of deep enjoyment and relaxation. Our sayings reflect how meals are more than just food, for example: *the family that eats together stays together*; and a rather lovely Latvian proverb I came across, *a smiling face is half the meal*. In all cultures and at all times in history there are significant rituals involving food.

The peer pressure around lunch kicks off in our school days. If the phone rings before 8am in our house, it's almost certain to be about who is having school dinner or packed lunch. Particular ingredients in packed lunches get the collective thumbs up or down once they are at school; in younger years, sometimes the more adventurous ideas came home again untouched because classmates have chorused "Eeeugh" when the offending item was revealed.

Hopefully most of us grow out of that, but, as the comments reflected in the survey show, we do tend to end up doing what everyone else does for lunch in our organisation.

"In my early career I ate at my desk. This was partly because of the lack of decent facilities close to the office to eat your lunch at, but also reflected the individualistic culture of the organisation. When I changed organisations, the practice was for everyone to go for lunch together every day. So 10-20 people would walk to the nearby cafeteria most days to have lunch together. From your first day in the organisation you were invited along with the rest of your colleagues. In my current job, we have a nice 'common room' so most people bring their own lunch in and eat it with others in a communal area" (Researcher/consultant)

The culture is enormously powerful. Taking a lone stand against it can be difficult if not nigh on impossible.

I've heard many people talk about "making a real effort" to get away from their desk for half an hour, or get some fresh air. It truly is a real effort if you are surrounded by people who are giving off disapproving vibes that suggest you are doing something wrong, or calling you a part-timer or lightweight. Or even if they're not doing that, but they are simply not taking a lunch break themselves, it gives off a strong message about how things are done.

So what can you do?

The strategy

As elsewhere in this book, I am keen on the idea of experimenting with different approaches. Running a pilot feels and sounds more manageable in relation to changing habits than an all-or-nothing, go-for-broke-and-hope-you-are-right approach.

The great thing about many modern workplaces is the flexibility that they bring, with regard to lunchtimes as much as many other working practices. You don't have to go to a canteen and eat a stodgy three course meal when the factory shuts for lunch; there are probably very few people who even have this option any more although it was still quite widespread when I started my auditing career back in the eighties.

You will know, for your own working environment, what is or isn't possible in terms of experiments. It's pointless me suggesting that you take your team to a local cafe as you may work in a place nowhere near a local cafe, for example.

In terms of developing a strategy, for yourself and/or your team, what I do suggest is the following:

1. **Identify what is within your control** – question this quite hard. It's easy to make assumptions about what is in your control based on the peer pressure part of the equation (for example "I can't take longer than twenty minutes even though I am entitled to because no one else does"). This is a genuine pressure. But it might not mean it's completely impossible to try something else.

2. **Set up a pilot** – how long will you try your experiment for? (three months is a good starting point). How will you measure any changes, benefits or drawbacks, to the new approach? This information could mean you can make a business case if you have to.

3. **Don't be too ambitious with your experiment** – you could aim to have a new approach twice a week for instance. Don't go for something that you are likely to have to drop in week one. You can always build on it later.
4. **Enlist support** – if you are responsible for a team, try something that can involve team members. Don't force everyone, but get some enthusiastic champions; the peer pressure may work in a positive way that means the rest join in later. Or find a group of like-minded colleagues to join you. Best of all, get your boss to take part – or if you are the boss, this is a great chance to model behaviour for others (see the point below for leaders).
5. **Publicise it** – not necessarily front page news, but tell others that this is what you are trying, why you are trying it, and what benefits you hope to gain. It could even be that this becomes a valuable case study to demonstrate an element of working practice to the rest of the organisation, or could even be a platform for good publicity in your industry. There could be brownie points in it, you never know.
6. **Persevere** for the period of time you have set for the pilot. Or if it all gets thrown off course in the first week or two, re-think your pilot and try again. Make it less ambitious or try finding different support. Good practice doesn't always embed overnight (as we all know).

And a note for those who are leaders

If you are a team leader or business owner or director, remember how powerful your own behaviour can be on others. It's quite common to hear people in leadership positions say that they wish their staff would go home on time or take a decent break at lunch time; but they proceed never to do that for themselves.

Those of us who are parents will recognise how hard it is to put across an effective policy of "do as I say not as I do".

The same applies at work to a large extent.

"One cannot think well, love well, sleep well, if one has not dined well."
—Virginia Woolf (1882-1941)

When you look back to the way some enormously creative and productive figures in history have worked, and the things they have achieved, what they nearly all did was to create space that meant they could concentrate on their particular field of endeavour.

They did not rush about like headless chickens, leaping from one urgent task to the next. They delegated lots of the small stuff, and many were fortunate in having families and servants that meant all the domestic detail was taken care of without them ever having to worry about it.

But the likes of Shakespeare, Darwin, Florence Nightingale, Brunel, Einstein, Charles Dickens, Mozart (you can add to this list) usually didn't live lives as long as we can expect to and none of them had the technology we have. It took them longer to travel anywhere and all their books and letters were handwritten. Communication with others could take weeks. They couldn't research topics at the touch of a Google button.

Yet they achieved world-changing lasting legacies through their work.

And I wouldn't mind betting they all had lunch.

CHAPTER NINE – IN BRIEF

- Lunch breaks can be easily dispensed with in a busy working life, and this seems to have increased over time.
- Lunch breaks may be important for more than just nutrition: in addition, time, company, and a change of scene are thought to be important to longer term good performance.
- Ways of setting up pilot studies in trying new approaches to lunch time are discussed.

LEARN MORE

- *Nourish* by Jane Clarke. The title says it all really. An interesting book with information and recipes for eating well throughout different stages of life.
- *Bodyfoods for Life* by Jane Clarke. This book, an earlier one of Jane's, looks at various health aspects related to food. It has chapters on migraine, sleep, middle-age and stress amongst others.
- *The British Dietetic Association* web site has a variety of food factsheets which, I believe, are a good place to start for sound information on topics to do with diet and a range of health conditions, as well as facts around food and weight, and food and mood. www.bda.uk.com.

A complete list of references can be found at the end of the book.

CHAPTER 10
GETTING YOUR SPARKLE BACK

It's impossible and probably unwise to live every day as if it was your last.

Most of us would get our mates round, open a few bottles and throw caution to the wind. If it then turned out not to be your last day, you would be left with a colossal hang-over and a credit card bill to match.

Even if you're the sort to be more sensible than that, and enjoy a calmer and more considered last day, you probably wouldn't spend it completing your filing and preparing the business plan you promised your boss.

For these reasons, I am not advocating the "live each day as your last" philosophy that can accompany some of the more unrealistic (to my mind) positive thinking approaches you might come across in the self-help aisles.

I come back to where I started the book in some ways. What I am writing about is intended to help you (and me) make the most of the life we have, which involves being grounded enough to do our homework, chores and preparation whilst not becoming so bogged down with it all that we no longer have much enthusiasm for our work or leisure.

How can we increase our chances of loving the life we live?

This is your life

Lives have a way of getting more and more complex, especially the more senior you get in an organisation. Maybe there are sunlit uplands at the very top, when you are surrounded by people to sort out all the day to day operations (at work and home) but observing world leaders or captains of industry from afar would suggest it's not all a bed of roses, even with money and power. Anyway, most of us wouldn't know.

For most people the weeks turn into years and define a career partly by design and partly by happenstance. We end up jumping around trying to balance often incompatible demands on our time and attention. Sometimes we can fall into living a life on hold. It will become better once various conditions are met: the children are grown; the mortgage is paid off; a project is finished.

However, unless you believe in an afterlife, it turns out that this really is it. *This* is your life: with all its busy-ness, pleasures, uncertainties, anxieties and ambiguities.

I hope that this book has introduced a range of things that, taken together, can make a difference to our experience of that messy now. There often isn't a calm, logical, cause and effect relationship between these. Instead, I think it is more akin to knitting or weaving various elements together to create your best chance of a life well-lived.

The areas I have brought into this book are all different threads that can add up to something reassuringly *possible* I hope. None of them are likely to change your life overnight. Most require some work. There is not guaranteed happiness, although if you keep your spirits up you are more likely to experience happy times. But something more enduring can be gained.

Meaning, purpose, or working (and living) to a reasonable potential might all be ways of putting it. We all have different takes on this.

What I am convinced of is that there are many factors involved in giving ourselves the best shot at both enjoying our lives and being able to contribute in our best way at whatever we choose to do for a living.

I am using this last chapter to look at a couple of areas that have, for centuries, been used by people to get some perspective, and renew their energy and enthusiasm: the role of the outdoors and the arts. The scientific evidence for these is gradually emerging and consolidating, and I think that in time we will know, with some precision, what is going on in our brains.

Even without all that, for thousands of years people have known ways of accessing experiences that make them feel better. Ways that can help them feel calmer, stronger, more determined and more creative. Ways that can lead to moments of real happiness, and satisfaction, in the process.

That make them feel good enough to get up and face another day, whether hunting wildebeest, running a multinational conglomerate, or doing an ordinary job down the road.

Getting back in touch with simple pleasures

For this part of the book, I interviewed Rebecca Speight, Director for the Midlands for the National Trust. Often associated with big stately homes, the National Trust is going back to its roots of late to emphasise the value of the outdoors. Octavia Hill, one of the Trust's founders, wrote in 1883,

"I think we want four things. Places to sit in, places to play in, places to stroll in, and places to spend a day in ... we want,

besides, places where the long summer evenings or the Saturday afternoons may be enjoyed without effort or expense."

She was not from a well-off background herself (her father lost his money in a financial catastrophe, she was not well educated and she worked from the age of 14) so she had some credibility when talking about "ordinary" working people; particularly those without much spare cash and who worked six days plus a week. Some echoes with current times you might think.

The most recent National Trust handbook puts this in contemporary language. And it applies to everyone, whether you consider yourself to be an ordinary working person or not.

"We need places that can lift our spirits and help us to find a different rhythm in our lives. This kind of refreshment isn't a luxury; it's vital. Extraordinary places can give us all this."

Besides the stately homes, the National Trust cares for and protects 255,000 hectares of land of special importance and 709 miles of coastline. Plenty of this is accessible for free. An especial favourite of mine is the South West Coast Path.

Rebecca explained that the Trust's aim is to be as well-known for its role in relation to the outdoors as for its houses and history. With that in mind, they have set up Outdoor Nation, a project designed to research the impact of the outdoors on people and also how we use and interact with the outdoor space we have in Britain. A particular issue is looking into the apparent decline in enjoying the outdoors across age groups (and particularly children) and over generations.

The surveys the Trust carries out with its visitors reveal that many people do find peace and tranquillity in its property and land. Rebecca says,

"We aim to provide places for people to get physical and spiritual refreshment. The words many of our visitors use to describe the benefits they experience tend to reflect this."

An overview of the evidence linking well-being and the natural environment by Julie Newton says that "Many studies suggest that people use environmental resources for physical activity as part of their strategy for improving mental health (Mental Health Foundation 2000). There has been a substantial amount of research that argues that natural areas are actively pursued by people to restore themselves from stresses of everyday lives (Mace et al 1999)."

The National Trust's role in providing easy and safe access to the outdoors is important. As Rebecca says,

"People can be a bit nervous of the outdoors. What we provide is a stepping stone. You don't have to be able to read a map or use a compass. But you can still get to some relatively wild and remote places on National Trust land."

She goes on,

"Increasingly visitors use the outdoor space we have all year round. We have seen a big growth in what we call "explorer" families using our facilities and joining the National Trust. These are families who are interested in having a bit of an adventure together – bike rides, camping – that sort of thing."

There has been a rise in interest in the concept of "nature deficit disorder" in recent years too. Primarily concerned with children, there is mounting evidence that it is harming their cognitive and emotional development (as well as their physical fitness) to become further and further removed from the outdoors and natural environments. A seminal book on this theme is *Last Child in the Woods* by Richard Louv.

He doesn't stop with children. In relation to working adults he writes:

"Those with a window view of trees, bushes or large lawns experienced significantly less frustration and more work enthusiasm than those employees without such views ... [and]

those who had walked in the nature reserve [as a break from work] performed better than the other participants [whose break was reading magazines, listening to music or walking in an urban setting] on a standard proof-reading task. They also reported more positive emotions and less anger." (my square brackets).

Rebecca adds,

"The recession and complex working lives do make people think about simple pleasures. We have committed to providing a thousand allotments on National Trust land by 2012 and are on target to achieve that. There's a big rise in interest in learning about growing your own food, and the National Trust kitchens have been working in this area for at least fifteen years now with an emphasis on sustainable food sources for our cafes and restaurants. We're also restoring and using increasing numbers of walled kitchen gardens to grow fruit and vegetables."

Other organisations are, of course, also involved in helping people access the outdoors. You may not need an organisation at all, it may just amount to going out in your back garden. However you get there, or wherever you go, getting outside will help restore perspective and energy when you can feel it fraying. Not only that, it is likely to improve your performance at work (and elsewhere) which is ultimately more rewarding all round.

Writing this in the UK, of course we have to take the weather into account. A decent coat and boots help. And trying to frame the weather positively too – I like this quote from nineteenth century English writer, John Ruskin:

"Sunshine is delicious, rain is refreshing, wind braces us up, snow is exhilarating; there is really no such thing as bad weather, only different kinds of good weather." (or – *a modern paraphrase - there is no such thing as bad weather, only the wrong clothes*)

Taking yourself out of yourself

Stephanie Sirr is the Chief Executive of Nottingham Playhouse. Founded in 1948, the Playhouse has been one of the UK's leading producing theatres ever since, putting on a wide variety of drama, music, dance and comedy.

I went to talk to her about how the arts can help us to regain our sparkle.

"It is really hard for your worries to find space in your head when you are concentrating on something else. There is something about live art that is especially compelling I think."

Stephanie is convinced, and convincing, about the value of the arts in increasingly busy lives. She highlights the formal shared ritual of theatre going as an example.

"The lights are down, you are with other people, and you are all concentrating on the same event. If you're at home, reading or watching television, you can always stop and do something else or be interrupted. That doesn't happen in the theatre."

It is an experience that she describes as "providing punctuation in our lives". It starts and finishes at set times, you cannot talk or take phone calls or do anything else whilst there. Good arts experiences are completely absorbing, whatever form they take. In a 24/7 world where working environments never switch off, this can be very therapeutic.

As Stephanie points out, "Whilst "me time" in spas and so on can be very enjoyable, it is still possible to be worrying or thinking about something else even if you're having a massage or reading a magazine. Whereas many arts experiences require a commitment to engage that fills that space."

There is even some evidence that engaging in the arts can be linked with a reduced risk of dying prematurely (reported in the

Arts Council England research report, *Your health and the arts: a study of the association between arts engagement and health*).

It just took me away

The nature of what we engage with is also influential. Stephanie pointed out a particular example, a play called *Forever Young* which the Playhouse has put on twice now. I went to see it the first time it was on. I wasn't quite sure what to expect (it was set in the future, in a retirement home for aged actors, and starred several members of the panto's cast).

It turned out to be one of the funniest, most surreal and moving evenings I'd had for a long time. I clearly wasn't alone in that reaction.

As director, Giles Croft, said in a filmed interview, "Superficially it is entertainment but really it is quite a serious piece of work about the condition that old people are put into and how it's better for us all to rebel sometimes, to claim back part of our lives".

An audience member, on leaving the auditorium, was still laughing when he said "it just took me away". Stephanie reflected, "It's not pathos, it's acknowledgement that this is what life is like. And laughing and being moved by that for two hours seemed to be really rejuvenating for our audiences."

Catharsis

I rather like the description of catharsis as "emotional cleansing". That's what many people experience through the arts. Stephanie says,

"If someone is seriously stressed, sometimes the power of seeing someone else in a terrible situation in a play for example, can actually be a bit much. But it is also good to see something that makes you cry, or rage, but it is not actually your own experience. It seems very healthy, and can be very moving, to be wrapped up in someone else's experience.

"We marketed our current play, Oedipus, on the basis of "you think you've had a bad day, wait till you see this". There can be something useful in either witnessing a character overcome huge odds or there may be an element of *schadenfreude* if they don't. You may see your own experiences as not quite as bad by comparison."

A universal experience

With other forms of art, for example, dance, Stephanie talked about the universality of it.

"Dance transcends language; there isn't necessarily a narrative, the lighting is usually fantastic and good dance can be a multi-sensory experience. Maybe it uses a different part of the brain. We can all relate to human movement in some way."

And sometimes the sheer skill involved in some arts is inspiring in itself. The Playhouse puts on many productions that showcase a variety of skills but in particular, Stephanie remembered the dance group *Flawless* as well as *Circo de la Sombra*, as being captivating and very satisfying in the "razor sharp, pure entertainment" they provided.

Making sense of our own experience through stories is also a very important part of drama and other arts as well as in psychology and coaching. The classic plays are, as Stephanie puts it, "well attended because they are all about you. That's why they are classics." Shakespeare of course is one of the most well-known examples, writing universal stories that cross all manner of boundaries to still have relevance to so many people today. There is a comfort to be drawn from knowing that some things have been "forever thus", and that our own grappling with issues may not be so unique after all.

Sport, religion and more

I have not touched on other major areas of life in this book such as religion, being an avid sports fan and creative hobbies. I think that all of these things can fulfil some of the same elements I have been writing about, and can provide routes to the beneficial activities and habits that help to keep our spirits up.

I am not writing from a religious perspective. Whilst I was brought up attending a non-conformist protestant church, I haven't done so for years and do not describe myself as having a religious faith.

I do, however, believe that life can be about more than we necessarily understand or can explain. There is still a great deal of the world around us, and our own nature, that is unexplored. Human curiosity has brought us amazing insights and breakthroughs as well as some nightmares. No doubt it will continue to do so.

It is true that the world is a marvellous place, and also true that it is a terrible place. Great things happen and so do awful things, every day. You have to choose to some degree which things you give your attention to.

Loving the life you live

It is not possible to love the life you live for every waking minute. Everyone will experience down times, setbacks, wrong turns and unwelcome events.

Sometimes we face overwhelming demands, whether at work or elsewhere. Sometimes we are rejected or our best laid plans go out of the window.

When those things happen, it can be very easy to lose perspective. Our energy can dip, we can be flooded with anxiety, and our heads might be full of a circular set of thoughts that don't help much but we seem powerless to stop. We stop feeling enthusiastic about things that we might once have felt passionate and excited about.

There are no quick fixes. Bailing out in some way might work, but doesn't always. As the title of a book by one well-known mindfulness exponent, Jon Kabat-Zinn, says *Wherever you go, there you are.*

We have to get on with it all somehow.

I think the arts and the outdoors are two very broad areas that have been important in human experience for time immemorial to help us not only get on with it all but enjoy it.

To have a great laugh at things. To be creative in coming up with new perspectives. To share our experiences with others. To recover when we are exhausted.

To love the life we live.

CHAPTER TEN – IN BRIEF

- Achieving a good balance between activities that are grounded and those which are inspirational in some way is important in maintaining enthusiasm and perspective.
- I don't advocate living life as if every day was your last.
- This chapter explores age-old ways of getting back to simple pleasures and taking yourself out of yourself through the outdoors and the arts to recover your energy and "sparkle".

LEARN MORE

- Find out what's available to you locally in terms of arts and the outdoors.
- This is obviously not a complete list or unbiased review but to give you a taster, some of my favourites are the National Theatre Live broadcasts (which can be accessed all over the world) – www.nationaltheatre.org.uk/ntlive; Nottingham Playhouse www.nottinghamplayhouse.co.uk; Outdoor theatre company (nationally throughout the UK and parts of Europe), Illyria www.illyria.uk.com; and our local independent cinema, the Broadway, www.broadway.org.uk. Recently an umbrella organisation called *Spirit Nottingham* www.spiritnottingham.com has been set up to act as a gateway to the arts in the city. In terms of the outdoors, the South West Coast Path is an enduring favourite of mine, www.southwestcoastpath.com, and more details about the National Trust can be found on www.nationaltrust.org.uk.
- *Last Child in the Woods* by Richard Louv is a fascinating read about the role of the outdoors particularly in relation to childhood development.

A NOTE ON GIVING UP

I don't consider anything in this book to be very complicated, and I hope it is all practical. Some of it will seem like common sense, but as a psychologist, I am keen for received wisdom to be challenged to see whether it really is good advice. I am also fascinated by emerging evidence from the fast-moving field of neuroscience as to what is actually going on in our brains when we behave in certain ways.

Sometimes this does, of course, back up the advice we may have been given from our parents and grandparents, and their ancestors too, over the centuries. But sometimes our common sense view can be challenged; I am thinking in particular of the common misconception that our work quality is not greatly affected by a lack of sleep for instance – or that our circumstances are the most important thing in determining our happiness.

I have tried to base what I have written in sound knowledge (as far as we have it) about what works to help us get through the daily grind. And, in fact, to do more than that: to give us an optimum chance of enjoying, contributing to and getting something rewarding out of the daily grind.

Many if not all of the topics I have written about involve some aspect of developing habits or practising new approaches or skills. Much as it would be nice, there are no real short cuts to doing that. If you want to get better at something, you have to go through a learning curve and something of a pain barrier that is usually part of practising something even if you have a natural flair to start with.

Taking care of ourselves is a funny thing. For all the reasons I have discussed, it can often be the last thing on our full to do lists. We see this in New Year's resolutions, which are often about doing things that we know are good for us. They usually drift off the agenda by spring time, waiting to be renewed next year.

The Dip

Seth Godin is an American author and entrepreneur with a marketing background. An engaging speaker and writer, one of his books has particular appeal when we start talking about giving up. *The Dip* is a short book that I have found very useful.

It describes the stage when any new project loses some of its initial excitement and starts to become plain hard work. That probably familiar stage when it doesn't seem to be going anywhere or you hit various setbacks. I can certainly testify that writing a book for self-publication is a good example of such a project.

Deciding when and if to give up is critical. It is certainly not about never giving up. Sometimes giving up is by far the best thing to do.

But it is about being clear and conscious about giving up in a controlled manner rather than giving up as a knee-jerk reaction when things are hard going. It is about having criteria at the outset to be able to measure your progress and decide clearly about whether you have hit a dead end, in which case, a change of strategy is eminently sensible, or whether this is the creative tough patch that is well worth persisting through.

Decide in advance under what circumstances you will give up on a new project and when. Don't decide when you are tired, demoralised, lonely or scared.

Habits and experiments

There are various estimates as to how long it takes to establish a new habit. I would say most of the things I have been talking about in this book need to be given a good three months as a trial period. The New Year's resolutions are best made with a view to keeping going with whatever it is until Easter.

It means you have a good chance of experiencing some of the benefits by then. And it feels less daunting than thinking you have to adopt the new habit for the rest of your life. Once Easter comes, you can decide if you want to extend it for another three months. Or change the habit slightly in the light of what you've learnt in the first three months.

Another very useful approach is to see things as pilots or experiments. A three month pilot exercise programme, involving running twice a week and signing up to a 5k event at the end of it sounds much more manageable to most of us than joining a gym and intending to go four times a week for a year to reach break even on the cost.

Be very clear about what your experiment is, how you will measure results, and how you will draw conclusions.

Allow yourself to give up at the end of it (but not before) if you want to.

The chances are you won't want to because there are likely to be some measurable benefits that you want to build on. Three months of earlier nights, or better lunch breaks, or taking time for good conversation with key people in your life – are all likely to yield some productive results that give you real information and evidence that you can use as a starting point to build on.

I think the best way to use this book, or coaching in general, is to develop some good experiments in those areas that seem most relevant to you.

I welcome feedback on the book and how you might use it and have set up a brief questionnaire, called *Keeping Your Spirits Up – what do you think?* for your comments on this link: **http://www.surveymonkey.com/s/Q6PJKXQ**

Let me know how you get on.

REFERENCES AND FURTHER INFORMATION

Action for Happiness, www.actionforhappiness.org

Arts Council England (2005) *Your health and the arts: a study of the association between arts engagement and health*

Binnewies, C, Sonnentag, S and Mojza, W (2009) Feeling recovered and thinking about the good sides of one's work, *Journal of occupational health psychology* 14 243-256

Binnewies, C, Sonnentag, S and Mojza, W (2010) Recovery during the weekend and fluctuations in weekly job performance: a week-level study examining intra-individual relationships *Journal of occupational and organisational psychology* 83 419-441

Burns, D (1999) *The Feeling Good Handbook* Plume, New York

Bridges, W (2004) *Transitions: making sense of life's changes* Da Capo Press, Cambridge MA

British Dietetic Association, food factsheets, www.bda.uk.com

British Heart Foundation *Keep Your Heart Healthy* www.bhf.org.uk

Clarke, J (1999) *Bodyfoods for Life* Seven Dials, London

Clarke, J (2011) *Nourish* Collins and Brown, London

Covey, S, Merrill, A.R and Merrill, R (1994) *First Things First: coping with the ever-increasing demands of the workplace* Simon and Schuster, London

Cox, T (1978) *Stress* Palgrave Macmillan

Crane, R (2009) *Mindfulness-based cognitive therapy*, Routledge, Hove

De Bloom, J, Kompier, M, Geurts, S, de Weerth, C, Taris, T and Sonnentag, S (2009) Do we recover from vacation? Meta-analysis of vacation effects on health and well-being *Journal of occupational health* 51 1 13-25

Doidge, N (2007) *The Brain that Changes Itself* Penguin Books, London

Donaldson-Feilder, E, Lewis, R and Yarker, J (2011) *Preventing Stress in Organizations: How to Develop Positive Managers* Wiley-Blackwell, Chichester

Foresight Report (2008) *Mental Capital and Well-being* www.foresight.gov.uk

Foster, R and Lockley, S (December 2011) *Sleep: A Very Short Introduction* OUP, Oxford

Foster, R and Wulff, K (2005) The rhythm of rest and excess *Nature Reviews Neuroscience* 6 407-414

Frankl, V (1959) *Man's Search for Meaning* Beacon Press, Boston

Fritz, C and Sonnentag, S (2006) Recovery, well-being and performance-related outcomes: the role of workload and vacation experiences *Journal of Applied Psychology* 91 4 936-945

Gilbert, P (2010) *The Compassionate Mind* Constable, London

Godin, S (2007) *The Dip* Piatkus, London

Gump, B, and Matthews, K (2000) Are vacations good for your health? The 9 year mortality experience after the multiple risk factor intervention trial *Psychosomatic Medicine* 62 608-612

Headspace www.getsomeheadspace.com

Health and Safety Executive *Signs and Symptoms of Stress* www.hse.gov.uk/stress/furtheradvice/signsandsymptoms.htm

Health and Safety Executive *What is stress?* http://www.hse.gov.uk/stress/furtheradvice/whatisstress.htm

Hill, Octavia 1883, *VII. Space for the People*, pp. 89–90

Horne, J (2006) *Sleepfaring: a journey through the science of sleep* Oxford University Press, Oxford

Kabat-Zinn, J (2004) *Full Catastrophe Living: how to cope with stress, pain and illness using mindfulness meditation (15th Anniversary edition)* Piatkus, London

Kabat-Zinn, J (1994) *Wherever you go, there you are: mindful meditation for everyday life* Piatkus, London

Kegan, R and Lahey, LL (2009) *Immunity to Change* Harvard Business Press

Kreitzman, L and Foster, R (2005) *The Rhythms of Life: the biological clocks that control the daily lives of every living thing* Profile books, London

Kühnel, J, Sonnentag, S and Westman, M (2009) Does work engagement increase after a short respite? The role of job involvement as a double-edged sword *Journal of occupational and organisational psychology* 82 575-594

Langer, E (2010) *Counterclockwise* Hodder and Stoughton, London

Langer, E (1989) *Mindfulness* Da Capo, USA

Lazarus, R.S., & Folkman, S. (1984). *Stress, Appraisal and Coping.* New York: Springer

Linley, A, Willars, J and Biswas-Diener, R (2010) *The Strengths Book*, CAPP press

Louv, R (2005) *Last Child in the Woods* Atlantic Books

Lyubomirsky, Sonja (2010) *The How of Happiness* Piatkus, London

Martin, P (2003) *Counting Sheep* Flamingo, London

Mental Health Foundation (2010) *The Lonely Society?* www.mentalhealth.org.uk

Mental Health Foundation (2011) *Sleep Matters* www.mentalhealth.org.uk

Nagelsen McCormack, B and Yorkey, M (2000) *Fit for Over-40's for Dummies* John Wiley and Sons, Chichester

National Trust Handbook 2011

New Economics Foundation, Centre for Well-being, www.neweconomics.org/programmes/well-being

Newton, J *Wellbeing and the Natural Environment: a brief overview of the evidence* (2007) available on the Outdoor Nation website, www.outdoornation.org.uk

Office for National Statistics (2009) *Smoking and drinking among adults*

Office for National Statistics (2010) *Social Trends 40: How UK life has changed since the 1970's*

Office for National Statistics (2011) *Social trends 41: Lifestyles and social participation*

Olds, J and Schwartz, R (2009) *The Lonely American: drifting apart in the twenty-first century* Beacon Press, Boston

Olds, J and Schwartz, R (2001) *Marriage in Motion: the Natural Ebb and Flow of Lasting Relationships* Da Capo Press, London

Outdoor Nation www.outdoornation.org.uk

Physiotherapy: the Chartered Society of Physiotherapists, Fit for Work campaign, www.csp.org.uk

Pressman, S, Matthews, K, Cohen, S, Martire, L, Scheier, M, Baum, A and Schulz, R (2009) Association of enjoyable leisure activities with psychological and physical well-being *Psychosomatic Medicine* 71 725-732

Schwartz, B (2004) *The Paradox of Choice – why more is less* Harper Perennial, New York

Seligman, Martin (2006) *Learned Optimism: how to change your mind and your life* Vintage

Seligman, Martin (2011) *Flourish* Nicholas Brealey Publishing, London

Sonnentag, S, Mojza, E, Binnewies, C and Scholl, A (2008) Being engaged at work and detached at home: a week level study on work engagement, psychological detachment and affect *Work and stress* 22 257-276

Stone, D, Patton, B and Heen, S (2000) *Difficult Conversations* Penguin Books, London

Williams, M, Teasdale, J, Segal, Z and Kabat-Zinn, J (2007) *The Mindful Way through Depression* Guildford Press, New York

Willson, R and Branch, R (2006) *Cognitive Behavioural Therapy for Dummies* John Wiley and Sons, London

ACKNOWLEDGEMENTS

There have, of course, been many moments when I have wondered why I am doing this. No one asked me to write a book, it's possible no one will read it, and all the deadlines that I've been struggling with have been my own idea. This means that the support and encouragement from other people has been vital to the whole enterprise.

I would like to thank:

John, Jess and Bridget for putting up with it all; and encouraging me to keep going even when that has meant I've been somewhat distracted at times.

Eileen Parr for being the catalyst for the first draft. Without her prompting, this would probably still be something I was just talking about.

Francine Pickering for encouraging me to "be bold" this year.

My parents for consistently cheering me on from the sidelines and enduring some very long phone calls about it all.

The small band of critical friends who read the draft through and gave me invaluable feedback: Bob Mirams (my brother); Eileen Parr; Victoria Best; Jenny Swann; Max Krafchik; Claire Welsh; Elizabeth Mirams (my mum); Sally Fildes-Moss.

Russell Foster for sparing me an afternoon of his time and being so enthusiastic. This sprang from a chance conversation at a book signing (his book) at Cheltenham Science Festival 2010.

Many friends, for doing what friends do best; especially Jude Burnett and Dawn Reeves who listened and supported from both a friends' and writers' perspective.

Members of the peer coaching group and Sarah McNicol for repeatedly coaching me around this topic.

Everyone who agreed to be interviewed so that their stories and perspectives could be included in the book; without them it would be a pretty dry tome.

Kate Ferrucci of Quarto Design for making it all look great. Good design is never to be underestimated.

The authors whose work I have referred to. I have sought permissions and tried to contact authors and publishers as best I can; and to refer on to their original work wherever I can. I have acted in good faith that I am representing their ideas appropriately (and have had much encouragement from those that I have heard from for doing so). Please do get in touch if this appears not to be the case.

Lightning Source UK Ltd.
Milton Keynes UK
175578UK00003B/3/P